TOWN & COUNTRY

Elegant Weddings

BY STACEY OKUN

A FAIR STREET/WELCOME BOOK

HEARST BOOKS   NEW YORK

Contents

Foreword

A *TOWN & COUNTRY* weddings book? In a word, inevitable. After more than one hundred fifty years of chronicling weddings, dating back to the magazine's founding in 1846, we felt it was about time we gathered our collective knowledge and experience and put it between the pages of a hardcover edition—for posterity. Of course, traditions have changed in the past century and a half. Today, for example, being respectful during a ceremony might well mean silencing your cell phone—and a horse and carriage are novelties, not the only way to get to the church on time. Modern weddings pose modern problems. Extended families, stepchildren, divorced parents and all the attendant tensions that go along with these real-life situations are what many couples have to deal with. Keeping peace on what is supposed to be a bride's most beautiful day is not always easy—if it ever was.

But some aspects of a wedding have hardly changed at all: the pursuit of the perfect bridal gown; the inordinate time and massive effort required to plan a proper wedding; the choice of the invitations (not to mention deciding whom to invite in the first place); the seemingly endless search for a location and the right florist, caterer and musicians. Add to this the anticipation, the doubts and probably some tears shed from utter frustration and you have a typical wedding in the making—no matter what the century or, for that matter, the country in which vows are taking place. Some things are universal.

I have attended countless weddings in my life—as a guest, as a bridesmaid and, yes, as a bride. From the moment my husband proposed to me at the stroke of midnight in front of the Christmas tree at Rockefeller Center on December 25, 1981, right through to the last day of our honeymoon in Italy several months later, it was a precious period of time that I shall remember always. Never have I been treated so delicately by those I came in contact with—from sales clerks and clergy to my own relatives. I concluded that there is something about a bride-to-be that brings out the same sweetness people reserve for mothers-to-be. I savored every second.

The author of this book, Stacey Okun, was married in 1996. At the time, she was on the staff of *Town & Country* as a senior editor, with particular responsibilities for jewelry, health and beauty. I remember her wedding day vividly. Both the ceremony and reception took place at the elegant St. Regis Hotel in New York City. Stacey is a lovely woman to begin with, but on that day, she was simply luminous.

Despite the usual chaos preceding the actual day, weddings still bring out the best in most of us. We dress up for the occasion. We're on our best behavior. We try to put the bride and groom's best interests before all others. There is a genuine understanding of the significance of the exchange of vows. And everybody wants to have a good time at the reception—it's as if we feel that's the least we can do for the new couple as they embark on a new and hopefully long and happy life together.

To all those future brides and grooms who will read this book: May it ease your anxieties, elevate your expectations and help you to enjoy what should be an exceptional day, one you'll remember always. And for the rest, may it reinforce the meaning of love, commitment and celebration.

PAMELA FIORI
Editor-in-Chief, *Town & Country*

Introduction

TOWN & COUNTRY HAS covered its fair share of weddings since its inception in 1846. But not until much later, in the mid 1990s, did the magazine devote an entire issue to the subject. At that time Pamela Fiori, the new editor-in-chief, recognized that no matter how interesting and comprehensive the magazine's articles might be, readers always clamor to see—and be seen in—the wedding pages first. The next, irresistible step was a special wedding edition. It was wildly successful, so there was another. And another. And another. Now the February issue, devoted entirely to weddings, has become a much-anticipated *Town & Country* tradition.

Perhaps the wedding editions have been so successful because of our beautiful photography or our innovative ideas for entertaining. But the truth is probably closer to this: Like the best marriages, *Town & Country* and the subject of weddings make a perfect match. There are dozens of bridal magazines on the market, and scores of wedding books. But when *Town & Country* turns its experienced eye on a subject, it is covered in the most elegant and individual of ways. That's why we decided to devote a book to weddings. No, this is not a how-to book—although it provides great insights and an abundance of practical information. (Readers of our magazine have always known how to do a great many things with grace and refinement.) Nor is it just a pretty face. Inside, you will find the wedding covered reportorial style, with a comprehensive chapter-by-chapter breakdown that addresses everything from determining the guest list to applying the last touch of makeup. Each chapter is presented

with the utmost attention to detail, offering ideas, anecdotes, invaluable advice from high-profile experts (*Town & Country*'s top-secret sources now revealed), in-depth profiles and finally, etiquette lessons for these fast-changing times.

Over its long history of publication, *Town & Country*'s evolution has resulted in an amazing ability to adapt to change. Therefore, you can expect this book to address the unique aspects of staging a wedding at the dawn of the twenty-first century. Though it acknowledges tradition, *Elegant Weddings* also covers modern rituals—many born of an increasing desire to make today's wedding a personal statement of personal style.

Yes, brides do seem more decisive these days. And more sophisticated. As the young bride and antique jewelry expert Mara Leighton has so wisely said, "We've all been to so many weddings. When I was planning mine, I started with the question: How do you make your wedding your own?" Another bride, New Yorker Valerie Rozen, answered that question: "The only way I could see having a big wedding was to make it feel small. And the only way to make it feel small was to be sure that my husband and I were reflected in every aspect of it, from the flowers to the music. For us, it wasn't just about throwing a good or a beautiful party. It was about throwing our party."

That's another reason this book is unique. It gives voice to these women (young and not-so-young, first marrieds, second marrieds, and dare we say, even third-time brides) at vulnerable turning points in their lives, as they relish and relive and recall and reflect upon the experiences they share on these pages. Their stories reveal that personal style has changed a great deal since *Town & Country* started covering weddings. Today's brides are generally older than they were even a decade ago. They're extremely chic, professional and focused, and many are—along with their grooms-to-be—financially independent. Grooms are also increasingly involved in the planning, because they, too, are more mature and more interested in the kind of statement their wedding makes to their friends and colleagues. In addition, many couples now foot the bill for their own weddings—and therefore feel free to make all the major decisions themselves. That's not to say that parents don't finance weddings anymore. Many do. Or sometimes they split the cost with the couple or help pay for the honeymoon or a new home instead. And planning a wedding is still the ultimate mother-daughter bonding experience. At this emotional time in her life, a woman typically turns to her mother for advice regardless of who's paying for the wedding.

The brides and grooms are not the only ones who have changed. A significant difference in the wedding industry these days is the degree to which every professional involved is willing to customize his or her services. Today's weddings are as individual as today's brides. There simply is no cookie-cutter approach anymore. Not with talented florists like New York's Renny Reynolds delving deep into a bride's fantasies in order to make her own dreamy vision of the wedding garden a reality. Not with creative caterers, such as San Francisco's Paula Le Duc, going so far as to reproduce a groom's favorite dish from a local restaurant. And not with wedding photojournalists like Denis Reggie of Atlanta shunning the conventional posed wedding shot in favor of capturing the bride and groom in unexpected, candid moments.

Indeed, every cake baker, every orchestra leader, every makeup artist, every wedding-ring designer and, especially, every bride interviewed for this book tossed out words like *individual*, *unique*, *attention to detail*, *custom* and *personalized* when describing the perfect wedding. Fortunately for the demanding bride of the twenty-first century, all these professionals are able to meet every challenge with remarkable ingenuity. "I don't just provide the flowers for weddings," the West Coast event planner Stanlee Gatti says. "To me every wedding is an individual artistic challenge that I work on and work on until the finished product is a masterpiece." And every *Town & Country* wedding today seems a masterpiece in its own right—an event that may be ephemeral in actual time, but is eternal in memory.

After six months of planning with event specialist Colin Cowie, newly marrieds Candace and Richard Weitz danced their first dance on a hand-painted floor in the ballroom of the Beverly Hills Hotel.

Chapter 1
WEDDING PLANNING

Susan Fales and Aaron Hill exchanged vows amid the grandeur of Manhattan's Grace Church.

Turning the Dream into Reality

"THE VAN OSBURGH marriage . . . was the 'simple country wedding' to which guests are convoyed in special trains, and from which the hordes of the uninvited have to be fended off by the intervention of the police. While these sylvan rites were taking place, in a church packed with fashion and festooned with orchids, the representatives of the press were threading their way, note-book in hand, through the labyrinth of wedding presents, and the agent of cinematograph syndicate was setting up his apparatus at the church door."

EDITH WHARTON, *The House of Mirth*

THE TURN-OF-THE-CENTURY wedding Edith Wharton described in her best-selling novel is not all that different from those of today. The sardonic author, who chronicled the mores of society's upper echelons, knew that few weddings end up being "simple" affairs; the planning often requires the skills of a Hollywood producer—skills that many brides tend to acquire whether they wish to or not. Wharton, a very prescient writer, in fact could have been describing a modern marriage. The difference is that if the Van Osburghs held their wedding today, they would probably convoy their guests in Mercedes minivans, while the orchids festooning the church might be flown in by special order just hours before from a Brazilian rain forest. The press, or rather, the paparazzi, might circle in helicopters

hoping to get a glimpse of the festivities. And the photographer, snapping candid shots, would likely be accompanied by a videographer hired to turn the tapes into a finished film to be replayed on the VCR for generations to come.

A wedding like the Van Osburghs' has always been a big event. But what has changed is the desire for individuality. That invariably means choosing a surprising location, serving an unforgettable meal, using exceptional decorations, or seeking a distinctive sound: a children's choir for the processional, perhaps; a jazz band for the reception or an a cappella singing group to entertain guests when the orchestra takes a break. New technology, from climate-controlled tents to Internet gift registry, is augmenting the possibilities, too.

Never before have brides and grooms had more choices, and perhaps more freedom to make them. And never before have weddings been so detail-oriented and, frankly, grand. Nor have couples been so personally involved in the planning. Until recently, the mother of the bride made the decisions. Now, more often than not, brides emerge from the daze of their proposals with their own distinct visions. This new model of bride plans her weddings as ingeniously as she's plotted her career. So when she begins to turn that vision into a reality, she typically approaches the task—Filofax or Palm Pilot in hand—with the drive and know-how of a corporate CEO. And with extended families increasingly involved, the day is not exclusively the bride's anymore. The groom's parents may need to be included, especially if they are sharing the cost with the bride's family—and thus some of the planning responsibilities

Before a bride begins dressing, she should lay out her entire ensemble—dress, shoes, jewelry and, of course, her something old, something new, something borrowed and something blue.

as well. This means finding ways to make both sides of the family feel involved.

Of course, planning a wedding is never truly finished until the bride walks down the aisle. But the process is best addressed in stages so that it doesn't become so distracting that the couple and their families are unable to manage their everyday responsibilities. At each phase it is important to step back, take a breath and make sure you are doing exactly what you want.

Making the Dream Come True

WEDDINGS BEGIN WITH a proposal. But they often begin years before that, with a dream. Some brides know only that they want candlelight, or that they simply must wear their mother's dress; others have more fully developed concepts in mind. These initial desires, however, are the most important part of the process, and brides should take this once-in-a-lifetime opportunity to dream a bit. Too many get caught up in all the particulars and the frenzy of hiring the right people right away.

It takes much more than a dream, of course, to make a great wedding. And that other part is what confounds most brides. Even those who know exactly how they want their weddings to be can get overwhelmed when faced with making the decisions. There are a few key questions to ask at this point: What do you think makes a great wedding? What do you want people to say when they leave? It was beautiful? Elegant? Moving? That was the best time I've had in so long? Then it's time to get down to the nitty-gritty of planning.

One of the most important things to do in the first few weeks of the engagement after reality sets in is to determine the budget, which will affect every single aspect of the wedding. The other is to come up with the guest list. The size of your wedding has an impact on the entire affair, because it will likely dictate location, and location will set the scene for the food, decor and even entertainment. Selecting the setting is also a priority because its availability will determine the date of your wedding. An out-of-town marriage requires additional planning for lodging, travel arrangements and activities for guests (see Chapter 2).

Another decision to make early on is the time of day you want to be married. Many brides neglect

"Brides don't have to reinvent the wheel at every wedding. The love that goes into the planning is the most important thing."
—RENNY REYNOLDS, *New York floral designer*

to consider just how much impact the time has on the mood of the party. Sunday luncheon in the garden or a black-tie dinner? The former will likely be a more lighthearted affair, while a formal dinner establishes an entirely different atmosphere: Night weddings are more romantic because you can have candlelight and dancing, which never seem to suit a daytime occasion. Time of year also affects plans, because you must consider potential weather problems, and even where you want to spend your honeymoon.

Once you have set these basic parameters, there are many other equally essential, if less obvious, considerations.

Quality: Offering the best makes guests feel pampered, ensures elegance and emphasizes the specialness of a special occasion. Choose the best quality that your budget allows. One really excellent dinner wine, for example, is better than several lesser choices for each course of the meal. Or if your flower budget is limited, opt for fewer arrangements but make sure the blooms are exquisite. And remember that quality doesn't necessarily mean money; it also represents the time and effort you spend on details designed to make all your guests feel involved in the most personal day of your life.

Personality: Make sure your wedding reflects your own sense of self and your blossoming relationship with your fiancé. No one wants to have a stuffy wedding, but you don't want an affair that is so informal it seems neither festive nor proper. One couple who recently married in Manhattan, for example, found the balance by deciding to emcee their own wedding. Because they were constantly talking to their guests, nothing seemed too stiff or formal, and they were truly able to set the tone for the party. The bride even walked down the aisle blowing kisses. Asking a witty friend to make a toast or hiring a favorite vocalist to perform as a surprise for your new spouse are other ways to infuse the occasion with personality. Laurie Arons, a San Francisco wedding planner, once designed a reception for a couple who were terrific dancers. After they cut the cake, they danced a tango; the bride actually changed out of her wedding dress and into a long red gown for the exhibition. Everyone, says Arons, was "just marveling."

Logistics: Are there enough rest rooms? How will guests get from the church to the ballroom? Are the acoustics good? These sound like insignificant details, but often the most basic parts of the wedding are the most easily overlooked. If guests are coming from out of town, you will want to provide them with maps, as well as plans or suggestions for meals, entertainment, appointments at the local beauty salon for the day of the wedding and baby-sitting services for young children who might not make it through the entire wedding (or aren't invited).

New and Old Traditions: Don't worry about whether a tradition might seem corny or old-fashioned; if it means something to you, include it. Customs such as dancing the hora or the tarantella and throwing the garter or bouquet might go in and

"People have been to enough dull weddings. Couples are putting in the time and thought to make them extraordinary. I've had women say to me, 'I was in Bali; I loved the flowers there. Can we plan the whole wedding around Balinese flowers?'"

—MARCY BLUM, *New York wedding planner*

out of favor with the times, but they are currently making a huge comeback, so chances are you will be in style whatever you decide. Moreover, tradition is important because it lends a sense of ceremony and weight to the occasion. Starting a new tradition within your own family is another way to make a wedding distinctive. One of three sisters to marry in Connecticut, for example, was serenaded at her reception by her middle sister, who sang the same song that the oldest sister had sung to her at her wedding. At another wedding, in Palm Beach, all the men on the groom's side told inspirational stories about their own marriages at the rehearsal dinner. It was incredibly moving, relates the bride, to hear them talk about

what marriage meant in their lives and what lessons they could offer her and her new husband.

Emotion: Have a mother-daughter day at a local spa. Rent "wedding" movies (*Father of the Bride* or *Goodbye, Columbus*) to get into the spirit. Spend time with your officiant so that he or she can say things about you that really matter. Keep a diary, even if it just contains the notes from planning meetings; your daughter might want to read them someday. And couples of any faith might consider the Jewish tradition of spending a few moments alone after the ceremony to prolong the intimacy of the occasion rather than immediately losing each other in the flurry of well-wishers.

Florists filled oversize urns with freshly cut roses for the extraordinary San Francisco wedding of Mr. and Mrs. Brian Alfred Stein.

Why Hire a Wedding Planner?

ONE OF THE MOST important decisions you will make is whether to hire a professional planner. Wedding planners are often caricatured as neurotic, bossy individuals who behave with the militancy of an army colonel. The stereotypes couldn't be more incorrect, but it is still critical for a couple to spend interviewing time to find the person who is the best match for their personalities. Brides should "click" with their planners right away. After all, this is one of the most important times in a woman's life, and she shouldn't have to spend even one moment of it with someone she doesn't like.

Wedding planners generally charge a percentage of the total wedding costs incurred, which can range from 5 to 20 percent. For that fee they typically guide the bride and groom through the entire planning process, helping to book all the services involved, organizing the pace and overseeing all details, often until the moment the newlyweds leave for their honeymoon. A planner can also coordinate engagement parties, rehearsal dinners and post-wedding parties.

What can planners do for a bride that she can't

WHAT TO DO, whom to call—and when? The key to planning success is in thoughtful masterminding, ideally beginning ten months in advance of the big day. Here's a month-by-month guide.

FIRST AND FOREMOST

- Revel in your engagement. Refuse to discuss specifics until you have had time to clear your head. Feel out the groom regarding how much input he wants.

IMMEDIATELY AFTER THAT

- Determine the number of guests and the budget.

TEN MONTHS BEFORE

- If you are going to hire a wedding planner, do it now. It is best to have him or her on board right from the beginning.
- Interview florists, photographers and caterers (if your reception site doesn't supply the food) and listen to bands. In some cities popular professionals get booked a year in advance, so be ready to be flexible with dates.
- Book the location(s) for the ceremony and reception and set the date.
- Reserve the date with the officiant.
- Invite friends and family to be in the wedding party. Let them know at this time if they are going to be responsible for their wardrobe.

NINE MONTHS BEFORE
(and No Later)

- Hire the florist, photographer, videographer, caterer and band.
- Hold preliminary meetings regarding colors, themes, menu, music and custom details.
- Start thinking about wedding dresses. Find out when the new season's dresses will be coming in. Spring/summer dresses typically reach stores in October while fall/winter dresses arrive in March. If you are having a dress custom-made, start cutting out pictures from magazines for ideas and hire the dressmaker now.
- Register for gifts.

EIGHT MONTHS BEFORE

- Arrange for the cake. Make sure you have a tasting now (before you consider a pre-wedding diet).
- Choose a design for the invitations and programs.

SEVEN MONTHS BEFORE

- Order your dress and veil or head-piece. Think about accessories (shoes, bag, gloves, jewelry) and make sure to purchase them within the next few months. Don't leave anything until the last minute.
- Start planning the honeymoon.

SIX TO FOUR MONTHS BEFORE

- Meet with the officiant.
- Choose the bridal party dresses.
- Make sure the groomsmen have their required clothing in their wardrobe or find a rental shop for them.
- Make an appointment with a hairdresser and makeup artist for the day of the wedding; schedule a few practice sessions.
- Book accommodations for out-of-town guests.
- Shop for wedding bands.
- Finalize honeymoon plans.

THREE MONTHS BEFORE

- Send out the invitations at least six weeks in advance of the wedding; two months if you're expecting many out-of-town guests.
- Mail invitations for the rehearsal dinner and other parties.
- Prepare for the first fitting of your dress with the appropriate lingerie and shoes. If your dress isn't ready, don't panic, but make sure you have a firm appointment in the next week or so.
- Hold a second round of meetings with all vendors to finalize choices.

TWO MONTHS BEFORE

- Schedule a time for your photographer to take some pictures of you as a couple, so that he or she gets to know you.
- Get the wedding bands engraved.
- Schedule your tasting and firm up the menu.
- Send a letter to out-of-town guests listing information about the events and activities planned for them.
- Decide where the bride, bridal party and groom will dress.
- Determine the transportation needed to and from the ceremony, reception and honeymoon destination and make the necessary bookings (travel arrangements to hard-to-reach locations should be made as far in advance as necessary).

ONE MONTH BEFORE

- Finish fittings (optimally) and try on your dress with all the accessories.
- Hold the last round of meetings with the vendors and service providers.
- Take care of final details such as preparing escort cards, choosing gifts for the wedding party, writing and practicing toasts and picking up the rings.
- Send out schedules to the wedding party and staff.
- Schedule another run-through with your hairdresser and makeup artist.

TWO WEEKS BEFORE

- Devise the seating plan. Don't fight about it; if the music is good, people won't be sitting much anyway.
- Remind the groom to get a haircut.

WEEK OF

- Pack for the honeymoon and confirm all reservations. Touch base with all the vendors and confirm all details.
- Perfect your beauty regimen (see Chapter 11)

Congratulations, you're ready to get married.

Newly married Billy and Vanessa Getty shared a kiss at their Napa Valley wedding, which was planned by Laurie Arons and photographed by Eliot Holtzman.

well-known Los Angeles planner points out, the guests can't hear the ceremony when you have a wedding on the beach—and you probably can't carry off a dress like Diana's if you are not marrying a prince in a national cathedral. Everyone wants a wedding that no one has held before, but sometimes there is a reason no one has given it: It just doesn't work.

Equally important, planners typically have type A personalities, an obvious asset at a time when even the most organized women contract "bridal brain" (something like temporary insanity) and exhibit the telltale

do for herself? For one thing, they typically have hundreds of resources unknown or unavailable to most brides and can help sift through the scores of florists, caterers, bandleaders and photographers in the business to find the right ones. They may also be able to negotiate better prices because of their long history of working with particular individuals. What's more, the best party planners have the best ideas. The most daring and creative are making a name for themselves by throwing a certain kind of party in which their particular look is an essential part of the fun (see Chapter 4).

While talented planners keep coming up with good ideas at every decision-making point, they also provide a reality check. Frankie Berger admits she has had plenty of requests for dresses that look like Princess Diana's or for weddings to be held on the beach with the waves crashing in. But as this

symptoms, including forgetfulness and crying jags. To counteract the disease, Frankie Berger schedules meetings for her busy brides so they can view centerpieces, listen to a band and choose linens simultaneously. Her working brides prefer to block out three hours in one day for an edited showing of all the choices. Marcy Blum of Manhattan is known for creating precise wedding-day schedules detailing every hour. Planners even do a bit of counseling, helping to keep the peace between bride and mother, prospective in-laws or divorced parents. The right planner, simply put, is someone who takes on all the worries of the day and allows you to feel like a guest at your own wedding.

Even so, some brides hesitate to hire a professional because they think they might lose control. A good planner, however, will work closely with you and make sure you are as involved as you wish.

"The poor mothers of this generation didn't get to plan their own weddings because their mothers took care of everything and they're not getting to plan their daughters' weddings, either."

—NINA AUSTEN, *Dallas wedding planner*

Even if you don't use a planner, there is still much you can do to ensure smooth progress. Get a system in place to organize your plans—a three-ring binder works well—and keep meticulous notes. Make up a schedule like Marcy Blum's for all involved, detailing such important time points as when the bridesmaids, ushers and photographer arrive, when picture-taking starts and when the florist is to bring the bouquet to the bride. It is especially important to hold a meeting approximately a month before the wedding at the reception site to allow everyone to assess the space and discuss details with all the other vendors. The head caterer, florist, bandleader and anyone else integral to the event should be present.

Reducing Stress

ASK ANY FORMER BRIDE to recall the planning period of her wedding and she will probably admit that it was stressful. Weddings raise issues: family issues, religious issues, money issues. Peoples' feelings tend to get hurt. Not to mention that two families are joining together, whether they like it or not.

Weddings can bring out the absolute worst in people, especially brides. They get bridal brain, which skews their thinking; they can't function normally and they cry easily—very easily. Moreover, the malady is extremely contagious, affecting mothers, mothers-in-law, sisters and even some grooms. Psychologists who have studied this phenomenon (yes, they actually have studied it) attribute it to three factors. One: The pressure builds and the brides crack. Two: In even the

most functional of families, people can act a bit dysfunctional when they realize their daughter or son is leaving the nest for good and they have to share them forever with those people (their new in-laws). Three: The bride and groom get jittery as the big commitment looms ahead; it frightens them no matter how much in love they may be. Rather than rock the boat by talking about it, they reroute their emotions to focus on less important details and have a rip-roaring fight about something as trivial as not being able to seat all their college friends at the same table.

After a nuptial Mass at St. Mark's Episcopal Church in Washington, D.C., Tina Tamara Hamilton and Eric Kevin Easter shared their first dance as husband and wife at the Historic Lobby at Postal Square.

BRIDES WHO HAVE married before may often struggle to produce a joyful affair without the pomp and circumstance of a first "princess" wedding. Custom, in fact, suggests that a second wedding be significantly different from the first, which is why they are usually relatively intimate—perhaps an elegant dinner party—and why the guest list is usually limited to the closest family and friends.

There are often certain guests at a second wedding who couldn't possibly have been at the first: the children. Creating a place for them in the festivities goes a long way toward making them feel comfort-

Ellen and Howard Katz were toasted by their children at Le Cirque 2000, in New York.

able about the marriage. At Linda Dunay's wedding to jewelry designer Henry Dunay, their combined family of four children and three grandchildren were present, gave toasts and composed the wedding party.

Another second-time bride, whose grown daughter served as maid of honor, comments on the importance of making the occasion meaningful to all the people there. "We didn't want a circus," she says, "and I didn't want the same kind of wedding my friends were planning for their daughters." To her surprise, she found planning a second wedding was actually pleasurable. It's much easier to add a sense of whimsy that first-time brides are usually too nervous to consider, and even more important: You can invite whomever you want. "It's not your mother's wedding, and her friends don't have to come."

When things get out of hand, brides and grooms should take some time alone for themselves. The same Manhattan couple who emceed their own wedding, for example, traveled to France for ten days just a month before the ceremony. They came back completely relaxed, had their wedding and then took another week in the Caribbean.

Not everyone can get away from it all prior to the wedding, but there are certainly useful ways to alleviate stress. Most important, stay organized. When the things to do seem too overwhelming, make a list. Delegate responsibilities; brides don't have to accomplish everything themselves. Nor do their mothers. And finally, keep the peace. If you

sense an argument brewing, have all the parties step back and remind those involved that a wedding is supposed to be a joyful occasion. Come back to the fiery topic a day or a week later after everyone has cooled off.

Most brides and grooms recall their wedding as one of the best days of their lives, although few realize that may be because the days leading up to it were so dreadful by comparison. Therefore it's essential to savor the moment, like that instant when you try on the dress and know it's "the one." Planning a wedding isn't always fun, but the headaches are worthwhile as long as you take time to revel in the highlights.

Etiquette

When a woman gets married, she is not just gaining a husband, she is also acquiring a mother-in-law. The mere words can send shivers down a woman's spine. Mothers-in-law, in general, just do not have a good reputation. Don't let the stereotype ruin your relationship with yours. After your engagement has been announced, take your mother-in-law-to-be to lunch, ask her to reminisce about her own wedding and let her know exactly what kind of involvement you would like her to have in yours. Being straightforward and warm with this very important woman right from the start will stand you in good stead throughout your life. Grooms, take note: The same goes for you.

Wedding Style: Caribbean Chic

NOTHING IS AS romantic as having a wedding on an exotic and lush Caribbean island, far away from daily routine. Nothing is as formidable, either. Alix Noel was up to the challenge. This New York children's clothing designer held her wedding to investment advisor Philip Toub on Mustique, a secluded three-mile-long island with only one hotel, no florists, no bands, not even a hairdresser. The ceremony took place at the island's quaint but small Bamboo Church ("where we squeezed in one hundred seventy people," she recalls), and the reception was at the one hotel, the Cotton House. Virtually everyone and everything, including floral designer Barbara Paca (from New York), the minister, a group of female vocalists, a steel band, the hairdresser (all from nearby St. Vincent) and every last candlestick had to be flown in. "I knew it was going to be a big production. The island is tiny, and you have to bring people over on a boat that comes only twice a week or on a very small plane from St. Martin," says Alix. "But Philip and I just thought it made for the most incredible setting."

Because most of the guests would be staying for about a week, twenty-five houses were rented to accommodate everyone in comfort. Alix started sending shipments from New York to Mustique six months in advance and arrived ten days early to organize everything in the boxes according to each of the four nights of festivities. The island wedding went off without a hitch, but one detail couldn't be planned. "Just as we were saying our vows, a tropical rainstorm hit and then was gone in a flash," says the bride. "We felt sure that the shower had blessed everyone."

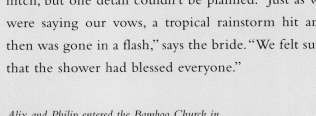

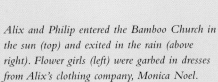

Alix and Philip entered the Bamboo Church in the sun (top) and exited in the rain (above right). Flower girls (left) were garbed in dresses from Alix's clothing company, Monica Noel.

An enchanting evening view of the Golden Gate Bridge beyond a pier in Sausalito.

Chapter 2
LOCATION, LOCATION

An empty airplane hangar in Brooklyn may not sound romantic—but it proved to be idyllic for Cynthia Rowley and Bill Keenan.

Choosing the Site, Setting the Scene

"WE WERE MARRIED in an old airplane hangar in Brooklyn, New York, that hadn't been used since the 1940s. The person who first showed it to us was shocked that we wanted it for a wedding: It was forty thousand square feet of space, completely abandoned, with no electricity. We brought in everything: tons of trees, one long table for one hundred sixty guests, flowers, candles, a stage for the band— and the night before the wedding, we hired a tractor-trailer to drag in the old 1940s DC3 that was still sitting on the airstrip. The whole place had a Casablanca feel. It was incredible. And because we got to create it, it was very us. My advice to brides searching for a location? Just because it's a wedding doesn't mean you have to forget who you are."

CYNTHIA ROWLEY, *fashion designer*

FEW BRIDES CAN BOAST of being married in an abandoned airplane hangar (even fewer would want to, for that matter). But because little in this world is unique anymore, it is not surprising that the statements people make with significant events are becoming all the more important. And because the location truly sets the scene for the entire wedding, it is imperative to choose the one that means the most to you. Often, the best is the most obvious—your home. As San Francisco wedding planner Stanlee Gatti explains it, using your family residence lends a personal element to the celebration. "Guests feel that they're much more involved with the family," he says, "and the wedding." Yet many other locations—a restaurant where you had your first date, perhaps, a favorite vacation spot, the house of worship one or both families have been attending for years—can capture that meaning, too. When Blaine and Robert Trump wed at the Marble Collegiate Church in New York City, their ceremony had personal significance because it was the Trumps'

family church. Dr. Norman Vincent Peale conducted the ceremony, which made the couple feel they were giving their marriage the best possible start. Certainly any wedding will be personalized by the toasts, decor and menu. Cynthia Rowley had her reception catered by a local Italian restaurant, offering such homemade specialties as ravioli, in tribute to her own Italian heritage and to the favorite food of her husband, Bill Keenan. "We're probably the only bride and groom who actually ate at our own wedding," she says.

Of course, no amount of personality will make your location great if you choose it without considering these essentials:

The Budget: Rates for any type of wedding are almost impossible to predict because there are so many variables. When settling on a location, always ask what is included in the fee and whether you will be charged by the head or by the hour. Plan for additional costs. At a hotel or club, for example, you will need to budget for lodging if you will be paying for any guest accommodations, and to plan for additional amounts for parking, alcohol and taxes.

The Guest List: The size of your wedding should suit the location and vice versa. Consider the ingenuity of the California couple who held their wedding reception for a hundred guests in the wine cellar of a Napa Valley vineyard where the groom works as a winemaker. Not only did the stone walls and barrels stacked up to the ceiling offer a setting with character, but the relatively

Billy and Vanessa Getty chose to hold their wedding at a private estate in Napa Valley so that they wouldn't have to limit their guest list. Left, guests enter the house for the ceremony.

With lush candlelight and one long table for 100 guests, the wine cellar at Sterling Vineyards in Napa Valley provided the perfect backdrop for the reception of a vintner and his wife.

food. Couples favor restaurants like the renowned Le Cirque 2000 in New York because they can count on such culinary landmarks to provide a superior meal that will set the tone and pace of the party. Sometimes a location is prized for its ballroom or amazing view, but offers average cuisine. Because the cost will probably include the meal, it is unlikely that the bride will be able to use another caterer for everything. In this instance, asking to bring in a special part of the meal from another source is a good strategy. That might mean hiring a sushi chef from a fine Japanese restaurant to give the cocktail hour a special twist. If the setting doesn't provide the meal and beverages, you will need to book a caterer (see Chapter 3), so be sure the location has space for a temporary kitchen.

The Look: Assessing how much work a potential setting for your ceremony or reception will need is crucial. If you do not have a wedding planner,

small room was the perfect intimate space where everyone could connect over a fine meal complemented by fine wines. The cellar, the bride recalls, also had a wonderful aroma. How many people can say that about their wedding location?

At the opposite end of the scale, the undisputed highlight of a hotel wedding is the grand ballroom that most large establishments have on the premises. Many hotels will give a range for the number of guests their ballroom can hold, but to know how many people can fit comfortably is even more helpful. In any setting, the most useful information is how many tables and how many seats will fill the space without cramping the dance floor. Guests should not have to squeeze between tightly spaced tables in order to mingle.

The Menu: The location choice also affects the menu, especially if the location provides the

The reception for Lela Helen Rose and Brandon Lee Jones's wedding was held at the Dallas Museum of Art.

> *"Where you have your wedding is a statement of who you are as a couple. The bride and groom should make sure to select a place that means something to them both."*
>
> —ANGELA MORGAN, *Dallas caterer*

Festooning the space with flowers would be overkill, so if a bride dreamed of creating her own look, a setting like this would not be appropriate. Having your heart set on a particular place may well mean adjusting the menu or the way you host the party to suit the space. If a location is too small for a seated wedding dinner, for example, consider having enough beautifully presented food passed to make a real meal and dispense with dinner tables and individual place settings.

The Outdoors: If a rainstorm on the day of your wedding is going to dash all your dreams, then you're probably not the kind of go-with-the-flow bride who should have an outdoor wedding. Rain, unexpected chill, a heat wave, wind—which can blow over flower arrangements or send the bride's hair into the air and the bride into a tizzy—and insects are all distinct possibilities for an outdoor event. In addition, these locations often limit the time of year you can hold your wedding. One compromise is to choose a setting with access to beautiful grounds. If the weather permits, cocktails can be served outdoors, and a formal dinner indoors.

The Courtesies and Considerations: The location should also be easy for guests to reach. If not, you need to provide transportation and/or parking or valet service. There should be plenty of bathrooms, a shaded area if the ceremony or

you might want to select a location that doesn't need a major transformation. Also keep in mind that a wedding at home often means extra work. Families usually wind up re-landscaping and repainting to give the house its best wedding face. If limited choices mean holding your wedding in a place used by dozens of other brides in your area, your job is to find a way to make the space seem new—by putting the band in a different place, perhaps, or having guests enter from a different door to give them a fresh perspective.

Though florists can do wonders (see Chapter 4), some settings are already so special that they require only simple decorations. That's true, for example, of the rooftop ballroom at the St. Regis Hotel, one of New York City's most fashionable wedding sites. Gilt-edged mirrors and impressive chandeliers make the room luxe to begin with.

For a summer wedding in a Southampton, New York, yard (above), the bride positioned a white tent over the dance floor and banquet tables—and also her swimming pool. Japanese paper lanterns were hung everywhere to provide romantic light as the sun set.

At the Napa Valley wedding of Lillian Wang and Baron Damian Schenk von Stauffenberg, guests dined under paper lanterns hanging from trees (opposite).

reception is outdoors and comfortable seating for everyone. All guests should have a view of the ceremony, and drinks should be offered quickly afterward at the cocktail hour. That means several bars stationed at strategic points and ample champagne, along with wine and water passed on trays. When guests must travel from ceremony to reception site, greet them with a welcoming glass of champagne. Each course of the meal should be served promptly, and music should fill the night with no awkward silences when the band takes a break.

There should be virtually no moments when something, even something subtle, isn't happening to ensure your guests' pleasure.

The Club, Hotel or Restaurant Wedding

CLUBS, HOTELS AND FINE restaurants have always been popular, and posh, sites for weddings. They are convenient because so many amenities are available under one roof: the space; the food and

The Chicago Cultural Center (left) is one of the city's most popular locations for a reception. To add drama to Mr. and Mrs. Brian Alfred Stein's reception in San Francisco's City Hall (below), a red carpet was laid on the grand staircase and urns of red roses were placed at the top.

beverages; the tables, chairs, china, glassware, flatware and linens; special lighting; the service staff; parking, and in the case of hotels, on-site (and often lovely) accommodations and a bridal suite. Country inns have most of the same features, but typically on a smaller scale. Country, yacht and university clubs also offer similar amenities, including catering and service staff, and often boast beautiful grounds. And though all are well-suited to receptions, they are also good locations for secular and interfaith marriages and tend to have educated staffs amenable to the special needs cultural customs may dictate.

Hotel weddings in particular can be grand affairs, because many are set in ballrooms with rich historical connotations: None could have a more romantic atmosphere, for example, than the St. Regis ballroom, where F. Scott and Zelda Fitzgerald used to dance. Another more practical attribute of hotels and of many clubs is that their staff includes a director of catering, who will act as a wedding planner within the confines of the location and is willing to meet with your florist, to help coordinate colors and to run tastings and rehearsals. The best hotels also follow current trends in cuisine and wine in order to provide the latest and most sophisticated service. Moreover, they offer valuable experience, partly because they are used to throwing the same party night after night. The seasoned maître d' is thus an expert at ensuring that your party flows.

There are considerations though. Older hotels, for example, were not always designed for quick and easy access, which can cost extra time and labor. Some hotels produce weddings only one way. But the best recognize that weddings are becoming increasingly extravagant, especially in decor, and are loosening up accordingly. If the staff is creative and flexible, they will set the tone for the party. They usually are willing to customize the space to your taste, to accommodate special lighting and power needs and to welcome decorations as long as the integrity of their ballrooms and other spaces is maintained. On-site catering directors will often agree to bring in alternate china and accoutrements, as well as to provide such extras as monogrammed napkins and matchbooks (at extra cost, of course). And finally, hotel and restaurant weddings can offer a dividend unavailable anywhere else in the world, except at that very place: the signature of a famous chef. At the St. Regis, Christian Delouvrier's highly praised restaurant, Lespinasse, sets the culinary

"If you are looking for the menu to make a statement, then choose a place where you know the food will be outstanding."
—S. MICHAEL ERESHENA, *Palm Beach events planner*

direction with a sophisticated nouvelle cuisine. At the Mansion on Turtle Creek in Dallas, the chef of note is Dean Fearing, highly touted for his equally elegant southwestern menus.

The Tent Wedding

PERHAPS NOWHERE ELSE can a bride customize her wedding as much as in a tent. Rather like blank canvases that can be transformed into great works of art, tents come in a broad range of sizes, colors, styles and looks, allowing you to "build" precisely the setting you desire, in whatever location you wish. A tent can be pitched anywhere: in a park or botanical garden, on the grounds of an inn, club, hotel or private estate or in the yard of your own family home. Tents offer flexibility, so you can have cocktails under one tent in the front yard, perhaps, then dinner under another in the back. Renting a tent means you can set your own pace for your wedding. And the setup can be used the following day for a post-wedding brunch.

It is not necessary to know the inner workings of your wedding tent or tents, but it is useful to be aware of some basics.

The bad news: Tent weddings are often the most expensive to produce because you must rent and supply everything, from fabric to filet mignon. Many brides dream of having a tent wedding in their backyard, but when they find out all the hidden costs this entails, they opt for a place that already has flooring, bathrooms, tables and chairs.

The good news: An enormous range of services and supplies are available to make a tent exactly what

Bride Kristin Tatham held her wedding at the Hildene Mansion— Mary Todd Lincoln's estate—in Manchester, Vermont. Perched on a hilltop and surrounded by mountains, the mansion has an extensive garden where, following cocktails, guests dined under a tent.

you want it to be. These include lights, generators, ground covering, dance floor, portable kitchen and cooking accoutrements, heat, air-conditioning and portable rest rooms. (No wonder the tent wedding is usually the most expensive to produce—and don't forget to budget in labor costs for all these extras.)

There are various kinds of tents and canopies that will make a difference to a look, so it's important to look at pictures or at the actual structures before choosing. Years ago, the only tents available for hire were white or striped. Today, you can also rent clear and black models. One of the most beautiful effects you can create is with a clear tent, which—best suited for a garden wedding on a gorgeous evening—can be lit by pinlights in surrounding trees for magical results. Of course, you need the gorgeous evening, too. And that can't be rented.

Tents themselves are not beautiful; the decorations and lighting transform them. Be prepared to bring in the flowers and perhaps even fabric for draping walls and ceiling. Palm Beach wedding planner S. Michael Ereshena covers every single inch of his tents, using fabric, shrubbery or lattice to conceal the exterior. The San Francisco events planner Stanlee Gatti once built a tent pergola covered with lemon leaves on a tennis court. Thirty thousand lemons hung from the ceiling, and a trompe l'oeil painting made the floor look like stone pavers with grass growing through.

Lemons notwithstanding, basic amenities are also necessary. Tents can be heated or air-conditioned and, yes, they are waterproof. Do, however, make sure the tent company provides a backup generator. The stoves, microphones, amplifiers, lights, heat or air all rely on having enough power. If one generator fails, the whole wedding could be ruined if there is no backup. Flooring is also essential; without it, high heels get stuck in the grass. You can also install temporary carpets or sisal rugs and even put down wood floors. For complete uniformity, carpets can be dyed—to match the bridesmaids' dresses, flowers or even the ribbons in the flower girls' hair.

And the weather? "You just have to have nerves of steel," says Renny Reynolds. This New York floral designer planned the only wedding ever held outdoors at Rockefeller Center, in a tent on the plaza. Plans called for only part of the area to be tented; the dance floor was uncovered. At five o'clock the clouds rolled in and the air felt positively stormy. But at seven-thirty, when the wedding was

"White is right" was the unspoken theme for this summer tent wedding, held in a private home on Lake Geneva in Wisconsin (opposite).

New York-based event specialist Philip Baloun prides himself on unexpected wedding decor. Unusual features of this tent (above) were its multi-color design and the soft draping of fabric in the interior.

scheduled to start, they blew away again. "The night was so beautiful, and between the lights, the wonderful backdrop of Deco buildings and the famous Prometheus sculpture, we all got goosebumps," he adds.

Even if inclement weather is forecast, the day is unlikely to be a washout. Tents come fitted with flaps that can be instantly rolled up to let in fresh air and rolled down to keep out wind and rain. When fashion designer Eliza Reed Bolen got married in a tent at the Connecticut country house of

her stepfather, Oscar de la Renta, the skies opened and rain fell steadily all afternoon. But gallant ushers escorted each guest to the tent under crisp white umbrellas, and the bride arrived standing up in a golf cart covered by an oversize umbrella. The afternoon picnic wedding went off without a hitch.

And keep in mind that in some cultures, rain on one's wedding day signifies good luck to come in the form of fertility. The more torrential the rains, the more children in the couple's future.

Creative Locations

ONCE IN A WHILE, you hear about those adventurous couples who get married underwater or in midair, skydiving, with a white parachute as the only nod to convention (the white, that is). That's not the norm. But it's increasingly fashionable to hold weddings at aquariums, historic mansions and private estates and in the public reception rooms of museums. Such locations provide an interesting backdrop for the ceremony and reception and an extra dollop of pleasure for the guests, who may even get the chance to roam a museum after hours during the cocktail party. Among the many distinctive interiors favored by New York brides are the spectacular lobby of the New York Public Library and the delegates' dining room at the United Nations. Settings ranging from botanical gardens to baseball fields offer equally intriguing outdoor options around the country.

There are caveats. At public and semi-public institutions in most cities, for instance, receptions are allowed but religious rites are forbidden, so the ceremony must be held elsewhere unless the couple is

Public spaces, such as New York's Museum of Natural History, provide an out-of-the-ordinary wedding backdrop. There, couples can dance under a gigantic blue whale.

being married by a justice of the peace. Also, couples often have to jump through hoops to obtain permission to hold their wedding at a museum or like institution; knowing a member of the board of trustees is always helpful.

If you are interested in a particular place, but are uncertain whether that spot has ever hosted a wedding before, or would be willing to, call the public or community relations director at the institution to inquire. Sometimes, access to private or historic estates may be obtained by making a donation, as is the case at the Streisand Conservancy, a beautiful stretch of land in Malibu owned by Barbra Streisand. At the turn-of-the-century Pratt Mansion in Manhattan, the fee goes to the Marymount School, which runs an elementary school there. Winding staircases and a view of the Metropolitan Museum of Art allow a bride to imagine she is a character in an Edith Wharton novel—for the small rental fee, plus the cost of the catering, in this case by the renowned Abigail Kirsch. That is the other restriction at such sites: It is often necessary to use the approved or resident

Getting There

YOUR CEREMONY IS in a church, your reception is in a private club across town. Why not make the trip in style? These days, couples who have two-part weddings are shuttling their guests from place to place with a dash of personality. Cynthia Rowley's Manhattan civil ceremony, conducted by Mayor Rudy Giuliani, took place at City Hall. When it concluded, two yellow school buses were waiting to take her guests immediately to the Brooklyn reception. "We served champagne and chocolate kisses on board," says Rowley, who actually hailed a cab with her husband, Bill Keenan, in order to share a few moments of privacy.

Meanwhile, the guests were singing on the bus.

Specially decorated shuttle buses can also do the job with flair. Or try something really different. Wedding planner Marcy Blum rents antique trolleys. They're old-fash-

Transporting guests in an original way makes even the moments between ceremony and reception noteworthy.

ioned and charming and they lend an elegant touch to a part of the wedding people normally don't think about.

After Melissa Biggs, an editor at *Town & Country*, wed financier Michael Bradley at a Manhattan church, most of their guests walked the few blocks in the crisp November air to the reception at the University Club. But Biggs and Bradley rode in style—New York style. They rented an old checker New York taxicab—the kind you never see on the streets anymore—because the back seat was roomy enough for the bride's dress. It was the consummate Manhattan wedding, taxi and all.

caterer. There may be additional limitations (restricting food and drink to certain areas, for example) designed to protect art and other property and the grounds. Certain institutions also request an extra fee for security guards and put a time limit on the party. Building and fire codes may regulate your decor (also true in hotels and restaurants), and an important exhibition could preclude use of the premises altogether.

All the hoop jumping can be well worth it, however. For one couple who held their reception at New York's American Craft Museum, the setting couldn't have been more perfect. The groom is an investment banker who paints as a hobby, and the bride was a graduate student in art therapy. In lieu of a table number, the guests' escort cards bore the name of a famous artist, and at the corresponding tables, a postcard of one of his or her famous paintings was set among the flowers. Guests had the run of the museum that night and enjoyed a beautiful glass exhibit. The only restrictions: no potted plants and no candles. "We dimmed the lights," the bride recalls, "and made do."

The Destination Wedding

A DESTINATION WEDDING can be exotic, extravagant and a vacation for the couple and their guests. For many, holding a wedding in a European country, on a Caribbean island or at a chic ski resort is a way of maneuvering parents into hosting a more intimate affair than a traditional country club or hotel wedding. Accommodations tend to be more limited and traveling is an expense, so the guest list is typically limited to the people who are closest to the couple and likely to make the trip. This can also make the wedding more meaningful.

The atmosphere and scenery of a destination setting lend a special character to the wedding. Peter Helburn, an Aspen wedding consultant, says couples are attracted to the Colorado resort precisely because they really want the "Aspen feel." They're not trying to create Los Angeles or New York in the Rockies. They want local flora, such as wildflowers, gerbera daisies, sweet peas and hydrangeas. The menu often includes game or trout.

Gondoliers paddled sisters and brides-to-be Jennifer and Neena Beber to a centuries-old Venetian synagogue for their double wedding ceremony.

Matt and Lizzie Larock chose this incredible panorama in Aspen as the backdrop for their wedding.

"I love the concept of escape. For just a few hours in a bride and groom's night, they can be transported by virtue of the place they've chosen for their wedding."
—STANLEE GATTI
San Francisco special events designer

Atmosphere is great, but what about the basics? Destination weddings require a focused strategy. Because of the distance involved, couples must usually turn over most of the planning to a wedding consultant or on-site coordinator, because the bride simply can't be in two places at one time. The consultant will meet with the bride a few times prior to the wedding, getting approval on colors and seating arrangements via phone, fax, mail, express service or e-mail. At almost any destination, the couple should be prepared for numerous calls and faxes back and forth during the planning stages and at least two trips to the location prior to the wedding.

A couple should also consider everything the destination does or does not offer before sending out the invitations. Are there appropriate places for the ceremony and reception? Good sources for food and flowers? Will language barriers be a problem? Because most destination weddings last through a weekend, be sure that guests have enough to do (pre- and post-wedding hikes, perhaps, or golf or horseback riding). Helping guests with travel plans and lodging and providing meals for them are other important considerations.

One New York couple who married at the Vatican faced their own particular challenges when planning their wedding across the Atlantic Ocean. Though the bride and her Italian-born fiancé made several trips to Rome, they still had to rely on local family and friends for the planning. Faxes went out to a priest every Saturday night, but the Italian side was so laid back the couple never really knew where they stood until a few weeks before the wedding. Language was another barrier. Before the bride took an intensive course in Italian, her fiancé had to do most of the talking. But the anxiety was worth it. Walking out of the Vatican in her Vera Wang princess dress, she felt "as if I were in the movies," she recalls.

Etiquette

Out-of-town weddings can be a costly expenditure for the guests. To help them plan, include a separate card sent with, or immediately following, the wedding invitation, listing a variety of recommended hotels in every price range. Etiquette dictates that the couple and/or their families provide a welcome dinner for the out-of-town guests. The rehearsal dinner, traditionally hosted by the groom's family, usually serves this purpose, but if all out-of-town guests are not invited, cocktails and dinner should be offered at a separate location. When guests are staying at the same hotel where an evening wedding is to take place, a hospitality suite offering coffee, juices and simple sandwiches during the day should also be available, if possible. Holding a brunch or lunch for guests at a nearby home is an appropriate alternative.

Summer and Brooks (right). Guests were treated to a stunning view of the Golden Gate Bridge at night (below).

Wedding Style: Island Ingenuity

THE WEDDING OF Summer Tompkins, an accessories designer, to Brooks Walker III, an architect, was a spectacular autumn event likely to be talked about for years by the six hundred fifty guests who attended. For one thing the affair, designed by Stanlee Gatti, was the first to take place on Treasure Island, a former naval base only recently decommissioned and located a mile off the San Francisco coast. For another, Gatti, known for creative solutions, built a little "wedding town" spread over most of the island, with separate sites for the ceremony, cocktails and reception. To create an appropriate spot for the rites, he transformed a former forty-thousand-square-foot parking lot by ripping out the pavement and adding sod, cypress

Every last morsel of the delectable wedding feast was prepared by Paula Le Duc Catering in San Francisco.

trees and a gazebo. Reached by shuttle buses, the next destination was the reception pavilion, approached by a redwood path winding through a newly created pumpkin patch. From an outdoor cocktail platform furnished with sisal carpeting and wrought-iron furniture, guests proceeded down a series of steps to a multi-level tent boasting fourteen-foot-high walls. The tent was draped with chocolate-colored velvet to complement the harvest theme. "It looked like the most beautiful restaurant you've ever seen," recalls the bride. As fireworks set off from floating barges signaled the dinner hour, tent flaps were drawn up in a grand ceremonial gesture to offer the first full view of the take-your-breath-away interiors—just as the orchestra started playing. It was, says Gatti, a great dramatic moment.

The staff of Glorious Foods in New York preparing mango, lime, and grapefruit-Campari sorbets.

Chapter 3
THE WEDDING MEAL

Catering to Modern Tastes

"MY HUSBAND IS GREEK, so I got married in Greece, in a small town south of Athens called Olympia. Because I've planned the menus for so many American weddings, I wanted mine to be different—really traditional Greek food. The wedding took place outside, right by the ocean, and all my guests could see the dinner being prepared; it was truly a feast for the eyes and the palate. It was a very sensuous food experience."

CARLA RUBEN-AVRAMOPOULOS, *chef and event planner*

> *"Food is so important in our culture. To share that as an integral part of your wedding celebration is a really special thing."*
>
> —LAURIE ARONS, *San Francisco wedding planner*

EVEN IN THIS DAY of sophisticated dining, it is remarkable how many people declare that their wedding meal isn't a priority. Poached salmon or filet mignon with haricots verts have been standard fare for so long that some brides don't realize that a run-of-the-mill menu is one wedding tradition they can do without. Indeed, food and drink are the traditional foundation of any celebration, and a particularly revealing measure of style and hospitality. The right choice can underscore a theme, establish the party's tone, add regional flair and enhance cultural and ethnic traditions. And, as at Carla Ruben-Avramopoulos's wedding, the food may even contribute to the sensuousness and emotion of the occasion.

Of course, ask ten different caterers what makes for great wedding fare and you will receive ten different answers. "Pasta at weddings is a thing of the past," proclaims Rita Bloom, a wedding planner in Washington, D.C. Yet Carla Avramopoulos, a chef and professional event planner herself, counters that pasta (homemade, of course) is one of her most popular appetizers. Abigail Kirsch, who creates menus for weddings at such smart New York locations as the Pratt Mansion, the New York Botanical Garden and the Tappan Hill estate in Westchester, considers cheese an important part of the cocktail hour (she serves it as a Boursin tart). But Rita Bloom flatly disagrees: "Why serve cheese in lieu of interesting food?" she asks.

In truth, there is no right answer. Not only have nationally celebrated chefs and a new crop of cutting-edge caterers transformed wedding food into a culinary art, but they have opened minds to the possibilities of incredibly innovative and varied

menus. As good wedding food becomes truly fashionable—and not a minute too soon—the cuisine naturally reflects an educated palate ranging from fish entrées such as red snapper and Chilean sea bass to distinctive flavorings like lemongrass and cilantro. Classics—caviar and smoked salmon—will always have a place. But you may also want to follow a hot culinary trend, like the current "grandmother nouvelle" cuisine, featuring signature comfort foods like mashed potatoes—served with an elegant veal tenderloin, perhaps. Ethnic dishes are another option. Consider, for example, the fashion for Pan-Asian

After the ceremony, Carla Ruben-Avramopoulos (opposite) was joined by her family on the church steps in Olympia. A Paula Le Duc specialty—a gold-leafed eggshell filled with lobster salad and beluga caviar and a silver-leafed eggshell with cucumber salad, topped with Sevruga caviar—appears at right.

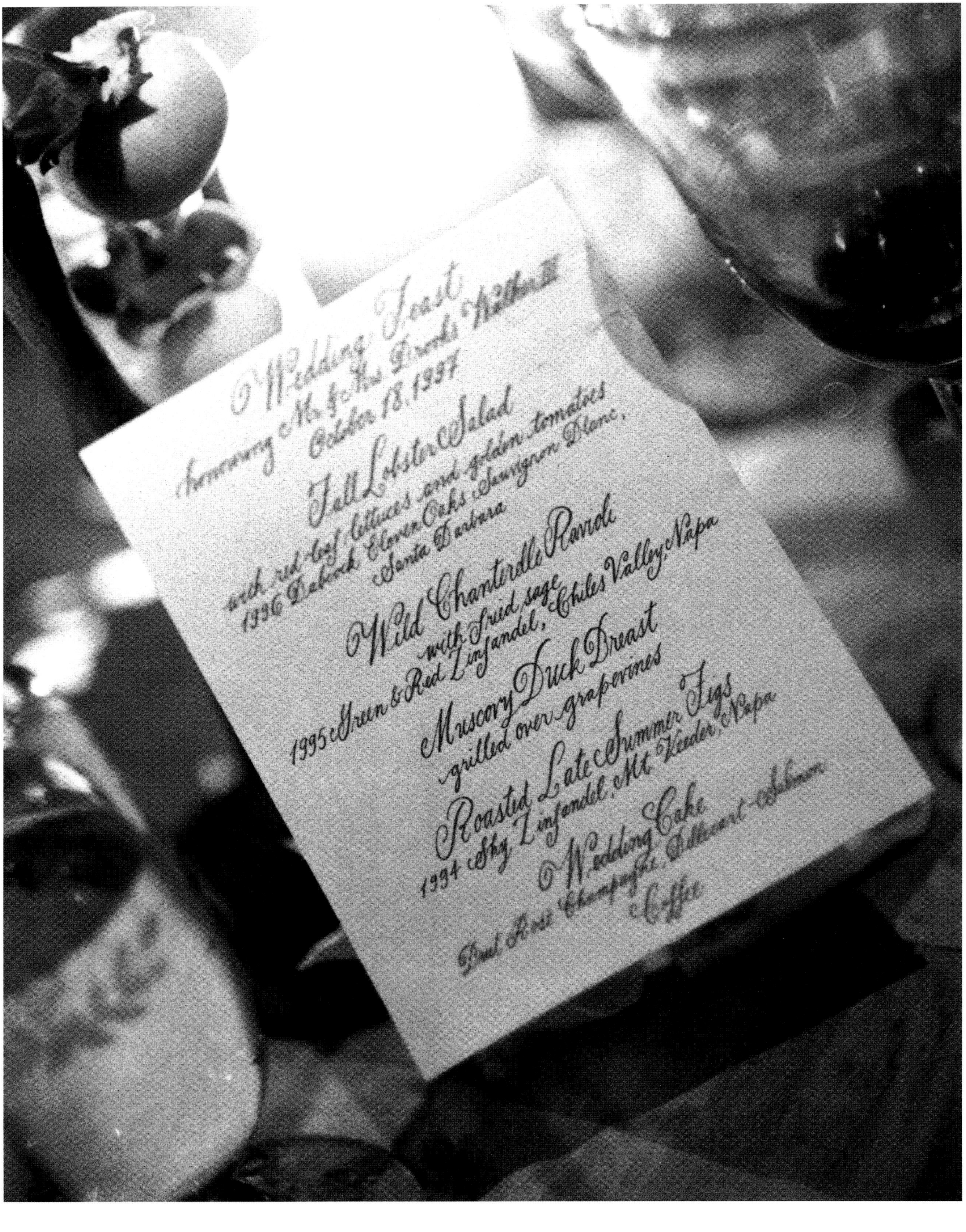

Wedding Feast

honoring Mr. & Mrs. Brooks Witter III

October 18, 1997

Fall Lobster Salad

with red leaf lettuces and golden tomatoes

1996 Babcock Eleven Oaks Sauvignon Blanc,

Santa Barbara

Wild Chanterelle Ravioli

with fried sage

1995 Green & Red Zinfandel, Chiles Valley, Napa

Muscovy Duck Breast

grilled over grapevines

Roasted Late Summer Figs

1994 Sky Zinfandel, Mt. Veeder, Napa

Wedding Cake

Brut Rosé Champagne, Iron Horse, Sebastopol

Coffee

Sushi, a popular cocktail hour hors d'oeuvre, is the inspiration for this serving of raw tuna wrapped in cucumber.

discussions regarding food and alcohol, the type of service, the number of courses and the pacing of the meal, dancing and entertainment. Make sure all your wishes are known and can be accommodated at the outset so there are no disappointments later. As for any party, the size of the guest list will help determine the menu. A responsible restaurateur or caterer won't take on a complicated meal for a big wedding because preparing large quantities of certain foods can compromise their quality.

Any chef or restaurateur worth his or her salt should also learn about your personal preferences. When a couple comes in for a tasting at the Bel-Air Hotel in Los Angeles, for example, the staff serves them the standard catering menu and then customizes the meal according to the bride and groom's reactions. Most hotels won't create an entirely new menu, however. People who choose to marry at a location like the Bel-Air tend do so for the acknowledged elegance and quality of the setting and cuisine, and they usually are ready to accept most of what the chef plans to serve. If you want more independence, you should probably hire a caterer, location permitting. Even if they are known for their own signature dishes, good caterers are willing to customize their menu to a particular bride and groom's tastes and will ask about their preferences.

One excellent approach to menu planning is to decide on the entrée first and build the rest of the

cuisine that is making sushi, dumplings and spring rolls so popular for hors d'oeuvres these days. Then too, the availability of the highest-quality fruits and vegetables year-round enables chefs to create summer dishes in winter and vice versa.

So, all things considered, there is simply no reason for pedestrian wedding food. The key to making the meal memorable and delectable is to imagine your wedding reception as a larger version of a party you would host in your own home. The simplest and best approach is to decide on a menu that you would like to serve—and eat.

Planning the Menu

START EARLY. Whether you are booking a club, restaurant, hotel or caterer, do so at least ten months in advance and immediately hold preliminary

A menu planned by San Francisco caterer Paula Le Duc (opposite) was handwritten and set before each place setting at the wedding of Summer Tompkins and Brooks Walker III.

meal around it. The goal is to avoid repetition. If a light fish is the entrée, a heartier appetizer, like an onion tart, strikes a good balance. Then be sure to have plenty of beef, vegetable and chicken hors d'oeuvres to complement the fish. Many caterers and hotel and restaurant chefs offer two choices for entrées. An alternative is a split entrée, known as a duet, which might include two small medallions of boneless chicken, with spinach and pine nuts, accompanied by a piece of fish.

The time of day your wedding meal takes place also affects the menu. A wedding brunch or luncheon might call for smoked or poached fish, light salads and beverages such as mimosas, or, depending upon the season, flavored lemonades. Typically less formal than a dinner reception, these affairs also accommodate the more casual presentation of a buffet as opposed to table service; guests tend to expect heavier fare when they are being served at a sit-down meal. The caterer Debra Ponzek, a former chef at New York's Montrachet

restaurant, once planned a luncheon for an outdoor spring wedding that included arctic char accompanied by potato and corn salads. Everything was light and absolutely fresh, with no heavy garnishes. It was, recalls the bride, who rode down the aisle on a horse, the kind of picnic lunch you would never be able to make yourself—and that was just the point.

Unusual wedding feasts notwithstanding, a formal sit-down dinner following an evening ceremony remains the most traditional and popular type of reception. The meal should be memorable, and engaging, right from the start. Carla Avramopoulos prefers to begin a classic wedding dinner with an attractive and interesting dish, such as her signature terrine of leeks, Portobello mushrooms and tomatoes, designed as a mosaic and topped with a white truffle vinaigrette and toasted black mustard seeds. "Starting with a salad is a fizzle," she says. "You can make it really pretty, but at the end of the day, it's still a salad." The entrée should be something homey and traditional, such as duck, fish or steak, prepared simply, but in a good-sized portion, with an equally simple starch and vegetable. Avramopoulos says the meal should end with a fabulous dessert that complements the wedding cake. Other chefs recommend light treats, with sorbets and fruits, because wedding cakes are now so delicious that people actually eat them (see Chapter 10).

And no matter what the menu comprises, wines and champagne are essential. When it comes to alcohol, don't leave anything out; a full bar should be open during cocktails, throughout the meal and after the cake cutting.

Lemonade served on silver trays (left) is a refreshing, and delightfully unexpected, beverage. A full bar (opposite) ensures that no guest will be without a drink in hand. At this Paula Le Duc event, even the bar itself is beautiful.

Make sure the wines complement the meal well, but have both red and white wine on hand because many people have a strong preference regardless of the food. Offering a wine produced the year the couple met or were born is a nice touch.

Looks Matter

BEAUTIFUL PRESENTATION is part and parcel of the wedding meal. Your guests come expecting something a little different and will appreciate food that is pretty and a little outside the norm. Presentation also works with the flowers and the table settings to set the tone. Guests may not be impressed by fruit slices passed on a platter, but they will remember the meal if the fruit appears in the fabulous topiary tree that makes weddings catered by Atlanta's Proof of the Pudding so special. Presenting food with flair might mean serving crudités in boxes crafted of wheat grass or setting off Asian hors d'oeuvres on a black lacquer tray. At one wedding dinner featuring an all-Asian menu, Paula Le Duc covered a serving table with moss and set out tiny steamer baskets containing

"If you serve something innovative, your guests will feel that they're experiencing something new, right alongside the bride and groom."

—PAULA LE DUC, *San Francisco caterer*

sushi, a dollop of wasabi on a leaf and a little pickled ginger. The guests, who could walk up and take away their own individual basket, were utterly charmed. The same San Francisco caterer has been known to present caviar in hollowed ice blocks. She keeps crabmeat cocktails, served in beer steins, cooling in ice buckets until the guests are ready to pick them up; the cocktail sauce goes in the bottom of the glass; the fresh crab is laid on it, and chives top it off.

Festive feasting (clockwise from top left): tiers of fresh fruit served al fresco at Billy and Vanessa Getty's reception; a terrine of leeks and Portobello mushrooms and tomatoes prepared by Carla Avramopoulos's Creative Edge catering; Paula Le Duc's heart cookie dessert topped with spun sugar; seared tuna offered by Abigail Kirsch at Tappan Hill.

Making sure the food is served at the right temperature is an important part of the presentation. Fortunately, improved technology makes it possible to keep almost any type of food appropriately hot or cold on a buffet table. And there are always creative solutions. Some caterers no longer use the traditional covered chafing dish to keep food hot because the interior gets too steamy. Le Duc is known for ingenious and attractive alternatives, like the heated marble slab she designed to keep such specialties as her quesadillas piping hot while looking pretty and appetizing.

The Spirit of the Party

THERE'S SO MUCH MORE to the wedding meal than the menu. The timing of the courses, the length of the meal, and the pacing of the dancing and the toasts are all equally important to consider. Pacing is so critical that you will need to plan exactly how you want your wedding meal to be served. Every hotel, restaurant or catering company offers its own methods and suggestions, but a knowledgeable staff will be flexible about the timing and presentation of the hors d'oeuvres and meal because they know these considerations are critical to the spirit of the party.

The traditional dinner wedding consists of a cocktail hour, followed by a meal of at least three courses: appetizer, entrée, and dessert/wedding cake. Brides who want their dinner reception to last find that a minimum of four courses, adding a salad after the appetizer, is a good idea. Extremely formal weddings tend to have a fifth course consisting of a palate-freshening sorbet served between the salad and entrée. However, many brides are opting for the simple—but no less delicious—three-course meal because extra courses drag out the time at table and may make the meal seem pretentious. The main question is how long you want your guests sitting at the table. Is dining the key to your wedding? Or partying?

Carla Avramopoulos believes both are. She recommends ushering the guests from cocktails in to dinner, inviting them to have one dance, then serving the appetizer and entrée. Dessert comes after a second round of dancing and the toasts. In this way, the guests can enjoy a meal without having to get up and down, and the "party" part of the party can also proceed uninterrupted. Brides who want to focus on the cuisine because they know their meal is going to be particularly special—perhaps because the reception is at a famous restaurant—may want to delay the dancing until after the entrée is served. This approach allows guests to savor the meal, as lovely music plays in the background, and eat the dinner while it is still hot.

One of the fundamentals of pacing the party well is the service. Have lots of it. A good wedding

"I like to think that the festive presentation of wedding food gives it a kind of thrill. The oohs and ahhs from the guests make the party all the more fun."

—CHARLIE PALMER
New York restaurateur and caterer

ONCE THE COUPLE and their caterer or chef have arranged the meal, they typically turn to planning the cocktail hour—an hour that definitely generates a certain excitement, perhaps because in real life we never get to eat pretty, bite-size morsels one after another. This is also the first chance guests have to greet one another, and if they are not seated together during the reception it may be the only time they have to talk.

What makes a great cocktail hour?

● Lots of food. And it should all come out in full regalia. When it does, it's a real crowd pleaser.

● Great food. By far the most sumptuous and exciting hors d'oeuvre is caviar. It's expensive, elegant, luxurious and enjoyable. Blinis and toast are a great tradition; newer serving ideas include such tasty morsels as oversize waffle potato chips. And accompanying the caviar? A vodka bar, of course—with different varieties (olive, lemon, cranberry) served in shot glasses.

● Variety. Offer a broad choice of vegetarian, low-fat (asparagus for the skinny people) and high-fat (it is a party, after all) hors d'oeuvres, along with some surprises (miniature lamb chops or the new wraps, like soft tacos). Passed food is essential, but make sure it is easy to eat; rule out foods like bruschetta (the tomatoes always seem to fall off). It's also great to have interesting food and drink bars. In New York, the hottest thing these days is the martini bar. In the Midwest, mashed potatoes served in brandy glasses are the trend; guests sprinkle cheese, caviar or onions on top. Shrimp, according to all caterers, is the magic word. As for smoked salmon—it's classic.

● Good service. People don't like to roam in search of cocktails and food. These should come directly to them—and quickly. Stock your drink bars with mineral water and soft drinks as well as alcohol.

● Action. Guests love to see chefs cooking up moo shu pork or preparing sushi. And it's always great to have a few of the musicians from the dance band playing in the background, as long as the music doesn't drown out conversation.

won't be a great party if table service lags and some guests are left to stare hungrily at others who are already enjoying their meal. The rule of thumb is to provide one food server for every fourteen guests and one bartender for every fifty to sixty. At a cocktail buffet, four or five waiters for every one hundred guests is recommended. Smooth and consistent service is essential, because a bumpy meal will interfere with the emotional high points of the reception—the toasts, the dancing, the cake cutting.

The type of service is also important. A buffet creates a less formal atmosphere and allows the guests to walk around and socialize during the reception. Another possibility is to have waiters serve the appetizers but to present the remainder of the meal buffet-style. A formal sit-down dinner, on the other hand, definitely calls for table service. The traditional style is French service, in which each part of the meal is served separately by a waiter, who makes up the diners' plates individually at the table. But many brides consider this very strict and formal approach too stuffy. The fashionable alternative is "plated" service, in which the plates are prepared in the kitchen, then brought out by a team of waiters who serve an entire table at once.

The service staff should be as unobtrusive as possible, neatly dressed in proper attire. This should go without saying, but check with your caterer about how servers will be dressed if they are not the regular staff at a particular location. One bride who had a country wedding went so far as to provide khaki trousers and white linen shirts for the service staff so that their uniforms would signal to the guests that the wedding was intended to be a relaxed, informal affair.

No matter how the meal is served, the key to the party's success is good flow. This is ensured by the all-important concept of "layering," meaning that guests proceed seamlessly and naturally from cocktails through the cake cutting without really noticing, even if they are moving from one room to another. If possible, serve cocktails in one location and the main meal in another. This underscores the importance of dining as part of the celebration, and emphasizes the impact of the decorations when the guests finally enter the tent or reception room. In any case, ample food and drinks should be provided each step of the way. At Paula Le Duc weddings, guests are offered champagne and strawberries before the ceremony, cocktails immediately after, then dinner, all without apparent pause. Even on the dance floor after dinner, waiters pass miniature fruit–shaped sorbets on toothpicks that guests can pop into their mouths without breaking stride. The entire wedding is an incredibly edible experience.

After-Dinner Delights

MANY PEOPLE HAVE an unspoken understand-ing that it is time to leave the wedding once the cake has been cut. If they go at that point, however, they

At the Napa Valley nuptials of Jamie Alexander and Steven Tisch, the Mediterranean-style wedding meal was served in the lush olive grove at Beaulieu Vineyards.

*Personalized chocolates, like these from
Creative Edge Parties, add a sweet
touch at the end of the wedding meal.*

might be missing some more fine food and drink. Weddings rarely end after the cake cutting anymore. Looking to extend the life of the party, many brides are complementing their meals with after-dinner delights. Some caterers add platters of toasted almonds, fresh pears, baguettes and snifters of vintage cognac. In Chicago the custom is to place candy—usually toffee—on the table during dessert. In New York, petits fours are the norm. For the wedding that ends in the wee hours of the morning, the old custom of sending guests home with the Sunday edition of *The New York Times* and a bag of bagels is very much back in style in New York. If you think the party is going to end late, send people off with doughnut holes and coffee in a cup printed with newlyweds' names. Chocolates bearing the bride and groom's initials are a clever variation on the idea.

Once you have planned all those last touches, it is time to have some real fun. Schedule a tasting. This sampling of the wedding food, typically held a month before the wedding, is essential. It should include all the hors d'oeuvres that will be served, as well as wines and champagnes, along with the entire meal, except the cake. The tasting is the opportunity to ensure that the wedding meal has variety and is well conceived. This is the time to assess every single choice, especially the hors d'oeuvres. Will they drip? Will they be easy to eat? You will try to make sure the combination of cooking methods and foods is just right;

you don't want everything fried, or everything steamed, and you do want a mix of beef, cheese, chicken, fish and vegetarian offerings. To get a sense of the presentation, ask the caterer or restaurateur to lay out the china and linens and food so that you can see and taste everything just as it will be on the day of the wedding.

A welcome break from the stress of wedding planning, the tasting provides one other wonderful opportunity: It's a treat for the bride and groom, who may be so caught up in the occasion that they never get the chance to savor their own meal on the actual wedding day.

Etiquette

There are always one or two—at larger weddings, sometimes a dozen. Wedding guests, that is, who turn up their noses at all the dining options. These days, good hospitality means accommodating the special eating habits of people on vegetarian, macrobiotic or other diets. At least two kinds of substitutes should be available. They might include plain steamed vegetables with orzo or a more substantial vegetable plate seasoned with herbs (either option would work for a guest who follows a kosher diet). You also may want to have simple fish and chicken dishes on hand. Salad and fruit plates appeal to most people.

*A flower girl (opposite) carries a
plate of cookies at this country
wedding in Sussex, England.*

Wedding Style: Antipasto in Aspen

WHEN MONA LOOK can't find her husband, Tony Mazza, in their sprawling Tuscan-style home, he inevitably turns up in their three-thousand-bottle wine cellar. Mazza, a well-known Colorado real estate developer, is also a wine aficionado who has always loved fine food and drink. His home was designed to ensure the enjoyment of both (state-of-the-art kitchen, plus the wine cellar). His courtship of Look revolved around them. So naturally, when planning the reception, Mazza, who is Italian, wanted to throw a family-style wedding feast.

Or put another way, a "food extravaganza." That is precisely what Tony Mazza asked of the couple's wedding planner Peter Helburn, of Just Ask Peter in Aspen. While the bride concentrated on the guest list and her dress, Mazza and Helburn set out to plan the menu. "I don't usually work with grooms," Helburn says, "but unlike most of my brides, Tony knew exactly what he wanted." He wanted the popular Italian restaurant Campo di Fiori to prepare the wedding meal. Even though the chefs there don't normally cater private parties, they made an exception—Mazza just happens to own the building that houses the Aspen restaurant.

True to great Italian tradition, preparing such a feast meant emphasizing quantity—without, of course, sacrificing quality. Thus when guests arrived at the Elk Mountain Lodge for the ceremony, they were surprised to be greeted by the groom, presiding over a room filled with antipasto tables heaped with figs, marinated vegetables, Italian meats and cheeses. Although this abundant pre-ceremony fare

To give the feel of the feast to come, tables (left and opposite) were set with food and wine already on them. The bride and groom (above) at Elk Mountain Lodge.

might have been enough to satiate any appetite, it was only the beginning. At the reception, during cocktails, trays of bruschetta, grilled shrimp and other hors d'oeuvres were passed. The meal was served family-style, with waiters bringing heaping platters of food to each table. The feast continued with bowls of olives, followed by salad, followed by three kinds of pasta (porcini risotto, penne with vegetables and meat-filled tortellini), followed by a choice of roasted rack of lamb or baked sea bass. Dessert was tiramisù wedding cake decorated with grapes (of course) made of marzipan. And there was more: biscotti and chocolate-covered strawberries to add a delectable finish. All the evening's many wines were selected from Mazza's personal collection. And even the centerpieces fit the theme: sumptuous baskets of freshly baked breads, olive oil, herbs, and, with a nod to tradition, flowers.

Today's politically correct brides don't leave the church in a shower of rice (it's harmful to birds). Rose petals are a more appropriate—and romantic—choice.

Chapter 4

FLOWERS AND BEYOND

New York floral designer Preston Bailey's urn with a cascade of flowers.

Designing the Wedding Look

"I HAD THREE WEDDINGS, and flowers were an important part of each of them. But it was my first wedding in Washington, D.C., on April 12, 1918—I was just seventeen years old—that was the large and glamorous one. I can't remember the name of the reception hall anymore, but I do remember that Mother had fixed up the place with lovely flowers. Actually, 'fixed up' is an understatement. I even had flowers at the top of my veil, making a little crown on my head. There were flowers everywhere. You couldn't even see the room through all the flowers. It was completely transformed."

BROOKE ASTOR, *philanthropist and author*

WEDDING DECOR HAS COME a long way since Mrs. Astor's nuptials of 1918, when merely filling a room with flowers was enough to mark a special occasion. Today, flowers might still transform the place, but the settings are not always what they seem. Consider the wedding of a young Los Angeles bride with a penchant for cognac-colored roses. She was married on a pair of tennis courts. These weren't just any tennis courts, of course: They were the courts at the Beverly Hills Hotel in Los Angeles. And by the time her wedding designer, Colin Cowie, was finished, they weren't tennis courts at all.

Cowie, who wanted a sophisticated and elegant look, began by pitching a clear round tent, then approaching its decoration much the way an interior designer would. Chocolate-colored chiffon draped the walls, plush carpeting of the same hue covered the floor, and an eight-foot domed *chuppah* enveloped inside and out with hundreds of cognac-hued roses formed the breathtaking centerpiece. Even the musicians were styled to complement the decor: Four harpists, garbed in brown, played atop a clear Lucite stage. The occasion marked the first time in the history of the 1912 hotel that the courts had ever been used for anything other than tennis. However, the transformation was so complete that few of the four hundred guests—who could not be accommodated in the hotel's small garden—realized where they actually were.

A ten-foot dome, festooned with hundreds of cognac-colored roses, replaced the traditional chuppah *at the wedding of Candace and Richard Weitz, held at the Beverly Hills Hotel.*

> *"We all go to weddings in the same ballrooms dozens and dozens of times. I look to find a way to transform a room so completely that people won't recognize it."*
>
> —COLIN COWIE, *international events planner*

If talented professionals like Colin Cowie don't make the role of the traditional florist obsolete, their creative thinking and comprehensive approach certainly challenge it. Indeed, such impresarios are rather like interior designers whose settings just happen to be tents and ballrooms. Some focus so predominantly on the other aspects of wedding design, including everything from cocktails to cake cutting, that they hire traditional florists to work under their direction. If spaces are dull or need reconfiguring, they do not hesitate to add platforms, fabric, backdrops and carpeting to achieve a particular look. Finally, they put in the flowers, but as Cowie says, these are the "cherry on top." First, they must create the structure.

The real impetus behind this growing fashion for a complete wedding decor can be summed up in a single word: style. As the emphasis on interior decoration and the demand for greater sophistication at home extends more and more to parties, people want their events to be very personal statements. Brides are making even the most traditional settings, such as chapels, reception halls and country clubs, unique through imaginative planning and attention to detail. Moreover, it is now also appropriate to choose unexpected locations for your ceremony and reception—the stone terrace of a California vineyard, perhaps, or the reception hall of a Chicago museum. These locales, however, may require particularly innovative ways to use flowers and other decorations. Though the scale or mood of such spaces might be perfect (how can you surpass a reception in the grand entrance to a museum?), certain aspects (the information desk, for example) may sorely need camouflaging. Why not do it with some flair?

Flowers, First and Foremost

FLOWERS HAVE ALWAYS BEEN one of the most important and traditional elements of a wedding. From the bride's bouquet to the altar and table decorations, they set the mood, express religious customs and transform a space with their colors, shapes, textures and scent. A bride often considers flowers first when envisioning the look of

To give their outdoor wedding an indoor touch, Jamie and Steven Tisch walked down an aisle adorned with an antique Oriental carpet.

her wedding. A wise approach is to ask a floral or wedding designer to walk you through a wholesale flower market so you can get a sense of the possibilities, from height and color to bloom type and fragrance. If this isn't possible, consult books or visit a nursery or botanical garden.

Narrowing the choice will likely depend on a number of logical factors, such as the region. Martha Harris, a Seattle floral specialist, points out that in the Northwest, where "everything is natural," locally grown wildflowers are fashionable. Seasonal availability also plays a role. But don't let your desire for a flower that may be out of season at the time of your wedding deter you if it is what you really want. Using lilacs or hyacinths during a dreary New England winter, for example, makes a lavish statement and evokes images of spring. Los Angeles

"Don't let anyone tell you that certain flowers are inappropriate for a wedding. If you love them, then they're appropriate."
—MARCY BLUM, *New York wedding planner*

wedding planner Mindy Weiss suits both the flowers and their arrangement to the season. She prefers tighter compositions for winter, filling unused floor space with pepper and birch trees for a lush feeling.

In the summer she favors looser, fuller arrangements for what she calls "an unkempt garden look." Using only one type of bloom, as did the California bride with cognac roses, typically provides a dramatic look. A mix of several varieties, such as hydrangeas, roses, and stephanotis, of different textures and heights, on the other hand, will yield a softer, more romantic effect.

Brides, however, need not be confined to such traditional flowers alone. A variety of new hybrids, such as freesias in hot colors like magenta, are now available. Berries and flowering greenery are another possibility. These used to be considered filler, but a talented hand can turn them into beautiful, unexpected arrangements. Or consider potted plants or fresh produce. At a recent wedding at the Four Seasons restaurant in New York, potted tulips lined the staircase, while baskets of fresh pears, grapes and apples bordered the famous pool, giving the space a sumptuous country air.

Above all, it is important to choose flowers that have some meaning to the bride and groom. People tend to be passionate about flowers. One Dallas bride was adamant that her florist rule out lilies because she detested the scent. Another, in Chicago, wanted only pink roses because those were the flowers her husband-to-be had always sent to

Small centerpieces can have a big impact: This tin bucket is filled with autumn flowers and surrounded by pomegranates—the fruit of love.

themes are de rigueur. They reflect the personalities of the couple and some aspect of their life together, their interests, their taste. Themes needn't be so comprehensive that every centerpiece, plate and petit four reflects them. Philip Baloun, a New York floral designer, finds the best themes in a word that represents a couple. Modern. Minimalist. Sophisticated. Traditional. Romantic. Historical. Architectural. International. He once created a Venetian wedding for a bride who was enamored of Venice. The canopy was designed to resemble a Venetian palazzo; the flowers replicated one of the bride's favorite rose gardens at the Cipriani Hotel.

her. A third filled the Sagaponack, New York, barn she used for her country wedding reception with cornflowers and sunflowers because they reminded her of childhood summers on Long Island.

Stanlee Gatti of San Francisco faced a recent challenge when a bride informed him that her favorite flower was the gladiolus, a gangly flower more typically associated with funerals than with weddings. Yet when the floral designer created five-foot-tall, umbrella-like centerpieces with two hundred fifty of the stems extending from the tops, he realized the gladiolus could be a very elegant flower. Most important, it meant something to the bride.

Melissa Rivers Endicott, daughter of Joan Rivers, had a December wedding at the Plaza Hotel in New York. Designer Preston Bailey transformed the ballroom into a *Doctor Zhivago* winter wonderland, complete with fifty-eight white birch trees,

Decorating with a Theme

OFTEN UNDERSCORED BY the flowers, a wedding theme usually starts with the kernel of an idea from the bride or groom. And these days,

This Santa Barbara couple sealed their vows amid a cascade of rose petals.

A view of the elegantly set tables and Sylvia Weinstock's seven-tier wedding cake (left) at the San Francisco wedding of Mr. and Mrs. Brian Alfred Stein. The couple shared their first dance (above) on the hand-painted rose dance floor.

thousands of tiny white pinlights, lush red roses and antique candelabra on the tables.

Sometimes something as subtle and simple as a color can be the theme. The classic white wedding is the perfect example, although many couples are updating the look by adding one strong accent color to the mix. The centerpiece at one all-white Boston wedding at the Copley Plaza Hotel, for example, consisted of glass vases holding a profusion of white lilies, roses and peonies. A turquoise sash tied around each vase matched those on the bridesmaids' dresses.

Colin Cowie's talent for matching the right theme to the right bride has much to do with fashion. He always asks immediately which fashion designers a bride fancies. Does she like Prada? Lacroix? Versace? The Los Angeles bride with the cognac-hued roses was Cowie's Prada fan, and as a

result, her wedding was very simple, very clean, very stunning and very, well, brown. It was an October affair, and the designer felt that the nontraditional scheme of cognac and chocolate—colors likely found at the Prada store in fall—would be extremely elegant. Because the bride loved the richness of brown, she did her entire wedding, from ceremony to reception, in those hues. Even the invitations were bordered in the color of the roses.

If an idea doesn't surface on its own, the best way to start planning the look and theme is simply to consider the season when the wedding will occur. Autumn brides can choose fruits, vines and dried leaves, for instance, for a harvest feeling. One bride used only red roses in terra-cotta pots set on rich red damask tablecloths at her December wedding at the University Club in New York. Each of the cherub-decorated candelabra on the tables held a dozen white tapers individually wrapped in ivy.

By far the most enduring, and perhaps endearing, wedding theme is garden-related. Many brides want to be married in a garden; when that is not possible, the right flowers, arrangements and accessories

A tight ball of roses and stephanotis complemented this bride's form-fitting Vera Wang gown (opposite).

Catch These Bouquets

A COLOR THEME, the look or type of wedding dress, and the other flowers chosen for the ceremony and reception all affect the choice of bouquet. These days, bouquets tend to be small. Just as wedding dresses are simpler, less fussy and more revealing, bridal bouquets are becoming more delicate. Some designers always suggest a nosegay because cascades can cover a beautiful gown. Besides, brides are usually nervous, so why give them something cumbersome to worry about?

Other popular bouquet styles include:

- Tight nosegays made of one type of flower (roses or lilies of the valley) or different flowers in the same color family (white with a hint of pastel)
- Diminutive topiaries held in hand
- Bouquets of fruit (little lady apples for fall, perhaps, or pomegranates and grapes for spring)
- Floral composites made to look as if the bouquet is a single oversize flower

Some brides hold vintage Bibles as their "something old" directly under their bouquets. One New York bride didn't carry a bouquet at all. Instead, she wore it. The small ball of roses and stephanotis on her wrist gave her the appearance of happily bouncing down the aisle. Bridesmaids' bouquets should be less significant than the bride's, but they might echo it, either through color or flowers, on a smaller scale. Tying a special ribbon (vintage or oversize, perhaps) around the bride's flowers also helps to distinguish them from her bridesmaids' bouquets.

Flowers "planted" in paper lanterns gave this imaginative Preston Bailey wedding at New York's Pierre Hotel an ethereal feeling.

can create the romance of a garden setting in almost any location, be it a tent, hotel, church or synagogue. Some botanical-theme weddings, in fact, boast more flowers than an actual garden.

The Elements of Wedding Style

FLOWERS MAY BE an essential element of a wedding decor, but they seldom stand alone. Establishing your wedding style and maintaining it from ceremony to reception depends on many other considerations that will make the ritual meaningful, the celebration memorable and the setting worthy of an elegant social occasion.

The Entrance: Few couples consider the entrance to their wedding setting, but because this is the guests' introduction to the occasion, the entrance is one of the most important elements. From the moment people arrive, you want them to sense they are part of something magical. At a recent wedding in the Rainbow Room, on the top floor of a skyscraper in New York's Rockefeller

Center, uniformed pages greeted guests on the ground floor. This thoughtful touch provided direction and added a sense of warmth and welcome to the corporate lobby. Floral arches and fabric tunnels also make innovative entries.

The Ceremony Decor: Regardless of their religion, many couples choose to marry under a canopy or floral arch simply because it is so pretty. These can be festooned with flowers or twinkling lights or decorated with candles. Softly draped fabrics, such as luxurious hand-painted silk, also make beautiful canopies and *chuppahs*. One wedding ceremony at the Asian Art Museum in Seattle took place under a streamlined canopy made solely of bamboo.

Ceremony decorations such as garlands, white aisle runners, bows tied to chair backs and votive candles are also lovely precisely because they are traditional. But don't be afraid to test your imagination. Altar arrangements, for example, need not be placed in the traditional urns. One New York floral designer suspends dozens of green plants draped with tiny lights from the ceiling above the spot where the rites will occur. Hanging antique chandeliers can also provide an unexpected touch.

Small details add to the richness of a well-planned wedding: candle holders that resemble the branches of a tree (right) adorned tables at Billy and Vanessa Getty's wedding; a simple ribbon with fresh flora tied around a napkin (below).

At outdoor weddings, the garden can be the perfect backdrop. Try something simple, using only outdoor candles in the spot where the ceremony will take place. Or take a cue from the location: One casual beach wedding for a couple in Santa Monica was held under an oversize beach umbrella draped with flowers; candles and seashells created an aisle.

Some hosts place cones of rose petals on all their guests' seats so that they can shower the newly wedded couple as they return down the aisle. Triggered by a gentle tug on a string, a simple device can be set up to sprinkle a couple with petals at the moment they kiss—most effective when the bride and groom don't know it is coming. The element of surprise is perhaps the most genuine special touch of all.

Setting the Table

BEAUTIFUL SETTINGS add elegance and glamour to the wedding table. Lovely tablecloths and napkins of fine linen or damask are essential. You can complement your flowers with candelabra, beautiful plates of fruit, crystal objects or anything else that has personal meaning. Simpler is always better.

Consider:

● As many candles—tapered or votive—as can comfortably fit on the table.

● Menu cards and place cards lettered in beautiful calligraphy. Menu cards, listing the courses and wines, should be placed on the plate, and place cards should be set directly behind the plate. These can be personalized in a number of ways. Martha Harris of Seattle did a wedding with a Provençal theme and made mini-bouquets of fresh lavender to hold the place cards. The guests could take home the lavender so the scent would always

remind them of the wedding. Harris also designed a party in a lemon orchard and used lemons wrapped in French ribbon as the place card holders. But be judicious: Whimsical touches should be added to the table only if they fit the mood and setting.

● Beautiful china and crystal. Hotels, country clubs and reception halls often offer limited choices, but you can always rent what you like from an outside source. Tableware should reflect the wedding style. Pottery is appropriate for an outdoor country wedding; elegant porcelain looks right at a more formal, indoor affair. For the ultimate in personalization, consider crystal wine glasses monogrammed with the couple's initials. Guests can take them home as favors, or the couple can save them as a set.

● Chair covers. Not always necessary, but when they coordinate with the linen colors, they tie a look together.

● Special touches. French-wire ribbon bows or ivy tied around the napkins or flowers tucked inside the napkin add whimsy to the table, depending on the flower. To avoid clutter, have waiters bring favors out on silver trays just as the wedding is winding down.

*"You would never have a wedding without flowers,
but flowers are not the only way to make an impact.
I've always looked at a party as an amalgam of elements."*
—RENNY REYNOLDS, *New York floral designer*

The Tables: Linens, linens, linens. "I can't tell you what a difference they make in the look of a space," says New York floral designer Bill Tansey, who maintains that linens add a much-needed layer of color, texture and quality to the tables. For a reception in a grove of olive trees at Beaulieu Vineyards in Napa Valley, for example, one bride set tables with custom-made linens in different jewel-tone colors so that they would "look antique, like tapestries." The only thing tying them together was the gold fringe on each.

As for table settings, Peter Baloun offers his own words of caution: "This is not your grandmother's wedding." Today, anything goes. Baloun uses everything from gold- or silver-leaf chargers to sleek glass plates in aqua blue set off on a crisp white tablecloth. "I did this at the Waldorf-Astoria once," he recalls, "and it was quite striking to see all the waiters carrying out the first course on these dazzling blue plates." (See "Setting the Table," page 75, for more tips.)

The Centerpieces: Avoid cookie-cutter arrangements. One alternative is simply to choose different containers for each table—a variety of cut-crystal and silver vases, perhaps. Whatever the choice, there is almost always a debate regarding centerpieces: low or high? To settle it, many florists recommend alternating low and high arrangements on different tables. At a seated wedding with dancing, it is best to put the taller

flower arrangements on the outer tables and the lower ones on the interior tables so that all the guests can have a good view of the dance floor.

Centerpieces, of course, don't have to be made of flowers. Sometimes grouping a series of candelabra can create a dramatic effect. Collections of crystal candlesticks—some short, some tall—or elegant silver objets d'art also make compelling compositions.

The Lighting: Lighting creates romance. Los Angeles floral designer David Mark goes so far as to say that brides who hesitate to commission lighting designs should consider that they are lighting art; they would never go into a gallery and see paintings that weren't lit. Like most professionals, Mark prefers to mix softly hued pinlights shining from above with natural candlelight on the tables. A less expensive option is simply to change the lightbulbs in the room to pink for a softer look and to set candles all around the space. Lanterns always add a whimsical touch; chandeliers, which can be rented, lend a

Tall vases of flowers, like Philip Baloun's (opposite) and Preston Bailey's (right), add drama and also give guests seated at the table the opportunity to converse.

Bubbles, Butterflies and More

RICE IS PASSÉ, not to mention politically incorrect (those poor birds). So what can a couple do to enhance the festivities? Bells or sparklers are great choices. Poured into miniature champagne bottles and placed on the tables, bubble liquid can be blown into the air by guests when the bride and groom make their entrance into the reception area. Releasing butterflies (sold dormant by mail-order companies) in an outdoor setting is another idea. When guests open origami envelopes on cue, the butterflies (pre-warmed into life) flutter upward. Wisps of color rise into the sky in a beautiful, ethereal, heart-stopping moment.

At one Maine wedding, something else appeared in the sky. Guests were served cocktails outdoors before an indoor banquet. As the sky darkened, a skywriter appeared and spelled out in script, "Dinner is served." Now that's a grand gesture.

lavish feeling. New York floral designer Renny Reynolds once hung hundreds of Japanese paper lanterns from the roof of a tent. Dimmers permitted him to make the mood more romantic as the evening progressed, as well as to spotlight demure bouquets of pink flowers on each table.

Lighting is also fabulous for that shift after midnight when an evening wedding goes from reception to late-night party, and the band kicks into more rollicking music. You are not going to switch the centerpieces, so lighting is the best way to change the mood. An expert can direct beams of light, for instance, to transform a ballroom into an edgy after-hours club. For evening weddings held outdoors, simple torches work well in the natural surroundings. The idea is to use a setting's loveliest features to best advantage. The bride who held her reception at Beaulieu Vineyards set her tables directly under the olive trees. The low branches were perfect for hanging lanterns.

The Clever Props: You wouldn't normally associate a living-room grouping with a wedding—unless, that is, you have been to a wedding planned by Mindy Weiss. This Los Angeles designer uses furniture groupings to create an entirely different aspect of socializing at a wedding by giving people a place other than their assigned table to mingle. Weiss's "living rooms" can work in any kind of reception space, from garden to traditional reception hall. They consist of two eight-foot couches; an

Maria and Parker Esse (above) left their Connecticut wedding in a flurry of bubbles. Bringing the indoors outside (right) is an increasingly popular technique for adding comfort and charm to a garden wedding.

armchair; two little French wood-back chairs; a coffee table topped with votive candles and a floral centerpiece (leaving room for drinks); and clusters of needlepoint pillows thrown nonchalantly on the sofas. The designer creates two such groupings in different looks and periods, depending upon the style of the wedding, and places them off the dance floor. Guests are usually mesmerized by the effect.

Trees and topiaries also create lush settings and are often used as borders to make a space feel as if it were enclosed in a secret forest. Scrims and other painted backdrops can be set behind musicians to create a focal point beyond the bandstand. Such scenery is typically painted in a style suggested by the wedding theme. Some brides choose to cover an existing dance floor temporarily with a personalized replacement, perhaps monogrammed or detailed with a geometric or floral border.

Personal belongings, of course, make the best props of all. At one Dallas wedding, the bride's father chose an eighteenth-century French painting from his extensive art collection to hang on the altar. The title? "Love Conquers All."

Gardenias and candles float in a pool, dressing it up for a wedding designed by Preston Bailey.

Etiquette

What happens to the flower arrangements when the wedding is over? Guests should never take home arrangements unless they are specifically invited to do so. Often the hosts save the wedding flowers for a post-wedding brunch and then discard them. Once all the festivities are over, they should be donated to a needy recipient. Contact a local hospital or nursing home to arrange delivery for the day after the wedding. Then request that your florist donate the time to deliver them by van. There is no reason that your wedding flowers shouldn't have a long, happy life, too.

Wedding Style: California Casual

SHE'S AN INTERIOR DESIGNER and he's the president of Williams-Sonoma Retail Division. They share a mutual passion for home furnishings and interiors, yet wanted an outdoor wedding. That is why Kendal and Gary Friedman brought the inside out at their wedding at a private Napa Valley estate, where they used furniture and accessories made by Gary's company to create an at-home feel on the sweeping grounds.

The magic began as arriving guests were led onto the estate by fourteen violinists clad in black tie, then crossed over the swimming pool on a bridge built just for the occasion. As they stepped off the bridge, they saw dozens of overstuffed sofas slipcovered

Floral designer Stanlee Gatti's imprint was evident throughout the wedding—from Kendal's ethereal bouquet (left) to the sheer white curtain that provided an enchanting backdrop for the ceremony (top).

One long banquet table wrapped around the pool (below), and oversize urns filled with dozens of oranges, lemons, and yellow roses placed throughout the property (left).

dinner table set with white plates, simple stemware, yellow roses and dishes of pears to accentuate the casual feel.

As the couple had hoped, their guests lounged in the outdoor living room before and after the meal, giving the wedding the homey atmosphere they were after. "I wanted people to stay at the wedding so that it would never end," recalls Kendal, who even provided a hundred chenille throws in case the evening turned chilly. "The couches were very comfortable, and people were so surprised and pleased to see them as part of our wedding decor," she recalls. "After all, there are usually so few comfortable places to sit and chat at a wedding. I'm sure that's why ours lasted until the wee hours of the morning."

in white. Set in a grove of oak trees, these comfortable seats were grouped around coffee tables topped with topiaries, bottles of brandy, and cakes and cookies. Winding around the pool was a single long

Mr. and Mrs. Charles Fra
request the honour of yo
at the marriage of thei

Anne There
to
John William

Saturday, the seven
Nineteen hundred
at three

Newman Hall - H
Dwight Way an
Berkeley

Chapter 5

WEDDING INVITATIONS

Pamela Fiori and husband, Colt Givner.

First Impressions, Lasting Memories

"I WAS THIRTY-SEVEN when my husband and I wed. We had both been single for a long time. Neither of us had been sure we would ever be married, so planning a wedding and all that this entailed seemed a little unreal to us. Until, that is, we saw the invitations. They were low-key and traditional, but there it was, in black and white. I'll never forget it."

PAMELA FIORI, *Editor-in-Chief,* Town & Country

WEDDINGS MAY BEGIN with a proposal, but many brides agree that reality doesn't set in until they see the words in print. One of the initial decisions you make in planning your wedding is whom you will include in the celebration. Think of it as the first stop on a carefully thought-out journey: Not only does your invitation honor the presence of your family and friends, it also lays the foundation for what guests can expect of the wedding. It makes the first impression.

And as every bride should know, first impressions count. The wedding invitation is an especially meaningful consideration because its design and presentation are so closely linked to our most firmly entrenched conventions of etiquette. The time-honored practice of delivering formal written invitations began in the mid-eighteenth century with European royalty, who customarily sent by a messenger on horseback a handwritten missive sealed with the family crest. The soiled outer envelope was discarded, and the clean inner envelope was then placed on a silver tray for presentation by the butler. Though its literal purpose is obviously outmoded, the custom nevertheless preserves an inherent sense of ceremony that seems especially appropriate to the occasion of a wedding. The traditional design, size and folding techniques for the

classic wedding invitation—which is still delivered in a double envelope—have remained fairly consistent since at least the 1800s and were firmly established with the 1922 publication of Emily Post's enormously successful book on etiquette. The classic invitation, sent six weeks to eight weeks before the wedding, remains by far the most popular type in America. Here are the essential elements:

The Paper: The finest is 100 percent cotton fiber (heavy stock), also known as cotton rag, which has a superb affinity for ink and is suitable for a variety of printing processes. The traditional hues are ecru and white.

The Format: The invitation is either folded and printed on the first page or designed as a single card. Regarding the latter, it has become popular and perfectly acceptable to bevel the edges and to add a black or gold- or silver-leaf border, or to leave a rough deckle edge.

The Printing: Printing from an engraved plate is the preferred method. Hand engraving is considered superior because it captures the most detail, but it is also the most labor-intensive and expensive engraving method. The accepted alternative is photo-engraving, which produces results that appear similar to the untrained eye. The typeface should be simple.

Mr. and Mrs. Duncan Laurens Frank
request the honour of your presence
at the marriage of their daughter
Barbara
to
Mr. Lyman Robert Straus
Sunday, the twentieth of June
at half after six o'clock
Temple Emanu-El
Fifth Avenue and Sixty-fifth Street
New York

Classic from Cartier: a formal invitation to a formal wedding at a Manhattan synagogue (above).

The Wording: The proper wording typically includes twelve specific lines, as follows.

Mr. and Mrs. John Smith
request the honour of your presence
(for a ceremony held at a house of
worship; note—*honour* is always
spelled with a u)
or
request the pleasure of your company
(for a ceremony/reception
held elsewhere)
at the marriage of their daughter
Mary Beth
(only the bride's first and middle
names are used;
the last name is assumed from
the first line)
to
Mr. Peter Miller Jones
(the groom's full name and *Mr.* are
used; this is his formal introduction)
Saturday, the fourth of May
two thousand and one
at half past seven
St. Regis Hotel
Fifth Avenue and Fifty-Fourth Street
New York, New York

Of course, slight variations are acceptable. If the reception is not at the same location as the ceremony, additional lines may be added to indicate the place and address ("afterward at the reception . . ."). Or a separate, matching card may be included.

This should read, "Reception immediately following the ceremony at (location and address . . .)." Consult a reputable etiquette book for further information on enclosures and the wording for special family situations.

The Envelopes: The outer envelope includes the full address—preferably in calligraphy. The unsealed inner envelope, which holds the invitation, is addressed with the guest or guests' names in the same calligraphy.

The Tissue: The original purpose of the tissue was to blot oil-based ink (which could take days to dry thoroughly) so that an invitation could be sent out without delay. Though modern engraving technology has eliminated the need, the tissue remains a part of the classic invitation. A delicate sheet of it covers the invitation in the inner envelope.

The Reply Card: Etiquette dictates that no reply card be included. The informed guest is expected to write a formal letter of acceptance or regret, in the third person, paralleling the wording of the invitation, on his or her personal stationery. Today, however, busy brides know that if they don't include the card, they may not receive a reply—ever. If you feel compelled to use one, the best design is a card engraved in the lower left-hand corner with a brief formal message that reads, "The favor of a reply is requested before (the required date)." Otherwise the card should be blank.

Traditionalists rarely stray from this format because it is the essence of good taste. Even when the most modern of women arrive at a traditional stationer such as Tiffany & Company or Cartier—with cell phones ringing and laptops in tow—they

Julie Holcomb designed Kendal and
Gary Friedman's invitation in the form
of a book that told the story of their
engagement and marriage.

admit they are utterly enthralled when they see the same invitations that women were ordering half a century ago. Nothing, they assert, says wedding in quite the same way.

Tweaking Tradition

OR DOES IT? Certainly the creative professionals who specialize in invitation design would disagree. Marc Friedland is one who prefers rich colors for the engraving—deep sapphire, cordovan, dusty gold and other hues that impart a ceremonial touch. Friedland, who also favors colored papers and unusual textures, urges his brides to personalize their invitations to reflect their own taste and sensibilities. "Quite frankly," as this sought-after designer puts it, "black on ecru simply doesn't give any sense of the event that is to come."

Some couples tweak tradition subtly. Wedding planner Elizabeth Allen, of New York and Atlanta, says the invitations she sends out are not elaborate or detailed, but they're still sophisticated. The only difference from the classic approach might be to substitute an especially fine paper imported from Italy. Los Angeles wedding planner Mindy Weiss likes to send traditional engraved invitations from Tiffany—with a twist. She ties a dainty satin ribbon around the upper left side of the inner envelope and puts the guests' names in the lower right corner. The invitation is still tasteful, she says, "but just a little offbeat, and a little more charming than expected."

Others throw tradition to the wind altogether. When actress Lea Thompson married director Howard Deutsch in a garden wedding, she chose a Friedland-designed invitation printed in soft green, edged in gold and mailed in an envelope lined with chintz printed in a beautiful abstract floral pattern. Kendal and Gary Friedman's five-page wedding invitation, designed by Julie Holcomb of San Francisco, read like a storybook of their romance. The first page was about the proposal, the second included the details of the wedding, the third described who would be in it, the fourth related planned events and the last served as an RSVP card. "We wanted to

Beautifully executed calligraphy; a motif, such as fruit on a vine, that is used on all the paper connected with the invitation; and elegant tissue paper are all touches that make wedding invitations feel luxe.

An increasing number of invitations are
fashioned to complement the wedding
design. The colors on the invitation are
thus likely to reappear in the flowers
and even the bridesmaids' dresses.

At home
Mr. and Mrs. Nicholas P. DuBrul
Post Office Box 2681
Aspen, Colorado 81611 USA
(970) 920-6824

Dr. and Mrs. Allen Park
request the honour of your presence
at the marriage of their daughter
Rebecca Ann
to
Mr. David William C
on Saturday the twenty-th
at two o'cloc
at the Earl Mill
on the can
the Cranbrook ?
Bloomfield ?

JOHN AND BEVERLY MILLER
JOYOUSLY INVITE YOU
TO THE WEDDING CELEBRATION OF
JILL LYNN MILLER
AND
CHRISTOPHER ANDREW HYAMS
SUNDAY, THE NINETEENTH OF APRIL
NINETEEN HUNDRED AND NINETY EIGHT
AT ELEVEN O'CLOCK IN THE MORNING
RITZ-CARLTON LAGUNA NIGUEL
DANA POINT, CALIFORNIA

FEAST AND MERRIMENT TO FOLLOW

> *"There are no rules today. Forget what Emily Post said that you can or can't do. My brides look at the invitation as an opportunity to make a statement of style."*
>
> —COLIN COWIE, *Los Angeles wedding planner*

Packaging and Props: Envelopes not required. At least one bride's beribboned invitations were sent out in slender boxes. Often, a wedding invitation will arrive in a packet along with directions, hotel-reservation information and invitations to the rehearsal dinner and post-wedding brunch all printed on coordinating paper. For a destination wedding, Ellen Weldon once created an invitation that included a card printed with these words only: "Call this number and we'll see to your flight and hotel plans." All the arrangements (and the bills) for the out-of-town guests were taken care of by the bride's family. Another creative invitation, to a Maryland wedding, was packed with "tickets" to

come up with something that was literally inviting," recalls the bride, "and that also said something about who we were."

In fact, almost anything goes. If you are a non-traditionalist at heart, consider the following:

Imported Papers: Invariably handmade, these can be incredibly beautiful. Invitation designer Ellen Weldon likes to use thick paper stock from Italy and ethereal Japanese papers hand-pressed with dried flowers.

Unusual Linings: A contrasting color, textured paper or lightweight fabric can make an unforgettable impression when the envelope is opened.

Ribbon: French wired ribbon is especially popular at the moment. Use it to tie a packet together or attach a small bow to the main invitation.

Colored Ink: Not unheard of these days. Hand engraving can be done in deep saturated colors as well as pastels.

Two Julie Holcomb designs (top) feature floral and bird motifs. Marc Friedland created this simple, yet elegant, invitation (right) for the actor Anthony LaPaglia, adding a ribbon and flower stem to give it the bucolic touch he and his bride, Gia Carides, were seeking.

Saturday, May 4, 1996
we experienced the most beautiful day of our lives
as we exchanged our wedding vows
upon the shores of Montego Bay, Jamaica
under the setting sun.

Keisha and Forest Whitaker

"Quite frankly, black on ecru simply doesn't give any sense of the event that is to come."
—MARC FRIEDLAND, *invitation designer*

various wedding events, including a tailgate party (the rehearsal dinner of choice for a sports fanatic), along with baseball hats and other sports paraphernalia to be used at the parties.

Special Flourishes: A family crest often appears on the classic invitation, but brides seeking unique and contemporary designs might also create their own insignias. One California bride being married for a second time chose an image of the Golden Gate Bridge for all the invitations to the various festivities, as well as for the reply cards. Marc Friedland prefers touches of nature, especially for more casual outdoor affairs. For a wedding held at a Los Angeles beach club, he adorned the invitations with tiny starfish attached to ribbons made of natural-colored netting. The invitations to an autumn wedding at a family winery went out with tiny clusters of brass grapes.

The Dress Code Decoded

STANDARD PARTY invitations often include a dress code for a formal affair, so why not wedding invitations? "Guests have a responsibility to the bride to dress well," says New York socialite and veteran wedding guest Blaine Trump. "And when everyone looks great, the party sparkles." If you are concerned about what your guests will be wearing, just put the dress information on the invitation so that everyone will be clear about what is expected, Trump advises. "Guests really do want to please their hostess."

Here's the lexicon—and some comments from the experts. (For less formal affairs, no code necessary.)

BLACK TIE. This states quite clearly that women are to wear evening dresses (short or long) and men should wear traditional tuxedos. "Pantsuits are not proper,"

says etiquette expert Letitia Baldrige. Nor is any other kind of suit. They're out of place. *Black tie* means a woman should definitely wear a dress.

BLACK TIE, LONG GOWN. Not common, but found occasionally. Joan Rivers, for example, used this very specific code on the invitations to her daughter Melissa's wedding at the Plaza Hotel in New York, because she felt dress was important to the overall effect of the wedding. "She put so much effort into the planning," recalls Blaine Trump, "and was worried that some of her guests wouldn't wear long gowns, which just seem dressier than short."

BLACK TIE OPTIONAL. "It's the worst phrase in the English language," says Letitia Baldrige. Of the same mind, Dallas socialite Lynn

Wyatt "looks in horror" at an invitation that includes this phrase. When it appears, she says, she never dresses up. Moreover, when most people see the word *optional*, they don't opt for black tie. Those few who do dress feel out of place, making for a very mixed up (and mixed-dressed) crowd.

CREATIVE TIE. Also distressing, says Baldrige. It further confuses. "An affair should either be black tie or not. If it is not, you need say nothing at all." John Anthony, however, is of another opinion. This fashion designer believes that an invitation stating *creative tie* signifies that the hosts want the guests to be more thoughtful and lavish in considering their attire. It might mean a patterned cummerbund for the man and a dress other than black for a woman.

Wedding Programs

WEDDINGS HAVE BEEN likened to live theater countless times. At a play, the theatergoer is provided with a playbill. And at an increasing number of weddings, guests receive a program designed to make the ceremony a more intimate experience for those invited. The typical example, designed to match the invitation, includes a cover featuring the bride and groom's names or monograms. Inside, it identifies members of the wedding party, the music and the sequence and meaning of the prayers and blessings, which is helpful for guests not familiar with the particular religious rites being celebrated.

Some couples also add notes and a few lines about the members of the wedding party ("Best friend since childhood" or "Met in college"). Others personalize them with pictures. One recent California bride who was wed at the Ritz-Carlton Hotel in Pasadena put a photograph of her maternal grandparents on the cover of her program. "I wanted everything about my wedding to have an old-world feeling," she explains. "My mother recalled that she had this incredible photo of her parents when they were in their thirties. Only a few guests knew who they were, but the picture said a thousand words to me."

Modern Language

THERE ARE USUALLY a couple of points in wedding planning when disagreements erupt, and invitation wording is often one of them. Emily Post's conventional wording is fine—as long as you have a conventional family. But which parents' names should come first when there are four sets of them? And should stepparents be included on the invitation at all? It's clearly a case for an etiquette expert (or, for that matter, a good psychiatrist). Wedding planners urge couples to be inclusive: This is a time for everybody to put aside family politics.

Another factor affecting invitation language is that some couples now pay for their own weddings. Because the first names mentioned on the invitation are traditionally the people who are throwing the

party, the bride and groom's names might now come first. Or the invitation might read, "Please join us in celebration of our marriage . . ." and conclude with the couple's names at the bottom of the page. And though you won't find it recommended in any etiquette book, including the names of the groom's parents on a wedding invitation is simply a thoughtful thing to do, according to many wedding planners. "It's kind and gracious to use the words *son of* following the groom's name," says Mindy Weiss. "It opens the doors of generosity."

This charming invitation (left) features photographs of the soon-to-be-married couple as children. For the invitation above, designer Ellen Weldon incorporated a picture of the groom's family farm—a favorite place of the couple as well as the site of the wedding.

Stanley Israel, Barbara Gorlikov, and Lisa Duprey
request the pleasure of your company
at the marriage of their children

Johanna Israel & David Duprey

Sunday the fifteenth of November
Nineteen hundred and ninety-eight
five o'clock in the evening

The Limn Gallery
292 Townsend Street
San Francisco, California

For a wedding held at a gallery, Los Angeles invitation designer Marc Friedland created this elegant design, featuring a simple gold frame with a ribbon and floral ornament.

record business; he's a movie producer) wrote their own clever copy about their fast-paced, high-powered lives. It went like this:

> On September 11, 1986, we made
> time for a date.
> Eight years and nine months later,
> he proposed. . .by fax.
> She accepted the next day. . .by phone.
> And now, after nine years, three hun-
> dred fifty-four days and twenty-
> two hours, our adventure in modern
> romance continues in person.

Other Thoughts— On and Off Paper

THE PERCEPTIVE WEDDING guest will note that an increasing number of invitations complement the overall wedding design. Often, the colors on the invitation reappear in the flowers and the brides-maids' dresses. Marc Friedland calls this the "visual vocabulary" of a wedding, noting that programs, escort cards, place cards, menu cards, save-the-date cards and thank-you notes should all look the same.

This trend can be taken to some remarkable extremes. For one California bride wed at the Beverly Hills Hotel, Ellen Weldon designed oversize cream-colored invitations complete with

Even when changing the language is not necessary, some couples do so to make their invitations sound more familiar than formal. One Los Angeles bride and groom who worked with Weiss mentioned to her that they had been neighbors when they were growing up. Weiss found a black-and-white photo of them as kids, hand-tinted it and made it the cover of the invitation. The only words on the front were, "It had to be you." A New York couple (she's in the

Etiquette

Change is good—at least for some people. As far as Letitia Baldrige is concerned, invitation etiquette is "in a shambles." She, for one, favors the strict, formal format of the classic wedding invitation. "It's a part of our history as a society that has always worked well," says the well-known etiquette expert, "and it doesn't need to change." If you are compelled to deviate, Baldrige advises, be sure the invitations are not so cute that they leave out important facts— such as the time and place of the wedding. Here are some additional tips from Letitia Baldrige for assuring that creative invitations live up to etiquette expectations:

- *Communicate properly, especially when you are not following the traditional format. Be specific about the festivities. If it's a dinner, make that clear. If there is only a cocktail buffet following the ceremony, say so.*
- *Put as much thought into the wording as you do into the design. Don't concentrate so much on the flourishes that you let typos and misspellings slip through.*
- *If you must use a reply card, don't forget to stamp the envelope. In this fast-paced world, people need all the help they can get.*
- *Do not automatically invite single people to bring a guest. Inquire first to avoid putting them in an awkward position if they don't have someone to ask. If you know the name of the guest that a friend will be bringing, put his or her name on the invitation.*

envelopes lined in handmade paper. Weldon worked with the bride's wedding planner, Colin Cowie, to ensure that the same colors, which included sophisticated copper accents, appeared on everything from place cards to sign-in book. Ultimately, Cowie hand-painted the dance floor in the same smashing style and colors as the marbleized envelope linings.

The four-step process took weeks to finish because each color had to dry before the next could be applied. "But it tied the whole wedding together from start to finish," recalls the bride. "It was a long journey from my invitations to dancing my first dance, but the invitations really started us out on the right foot."

Ellen Weldon's invitation package for Candace and Richard Weitz's wedding was printed on cream paper with touches of copper so that it would match the colors of the wedding.

Wedding Style: Cape Cod Casual

EVERYONE WHO WAS INVITED to Nicole Dawes's Cape Cod wedding expected that the invitations would have potato chips engraved on them. Not just any potato chips, but Cape Cod brand—the gourmet version of the classic American chip that was created and made famous by the bride's family. As it happened, there were potato chips: served at the pre-wedding clambake, included in the amenity baskets delivered to out-of-town guests and printed on the beach bags given to every guest. But when it came to her invitations, which would set the tone for the whole wedding, the bride was looking for something a little more sophisticated.

That's why she turned to New York-based invitation designer Ellen Weldon. Weldon, who just

happens to be the daughter of wedding-cake doyenne Sylvia Weinstock (see Chapter 10), has her mother's knack for creativity—the ability to produce something out of the ordinary that still manages to be refined, chic and terribly elegant. Like most of the best invitation designers today, Weldon uses only the finest papers, inks and calligraphy. And her ideas set her apart. After meeting Nicole, Weldon immersed herself in the details of the bride's wedding plans and took very seriously her request to send out a classic invitation with "just a little something special on it."

That something special turned out to be a symbol as simple and obvious as the scallop shells that are scattered all over Cape Cod's sandy beaches. A type of shell that Dawes grew up collecting. A shell that, used as a personalizing motif on her cream-colored save-the-date cards, invitations, menu and escort cards and wedding programs, symbolized exactly the kind of wedding that the couple was intent on having—summery, seaside and stylish—before anyone read the words.

There were words, of course: bidding guests to celebrate at the Wequassett Inn, where they dined on lobster ravioli, grilled shrimp and filet mignon at tables decorated with bouquets of native flowers—arranged in clear vases complete with a handful of scallop shells in the base. "I can't look at one of those shells today without remembering my wedding," Dawes says. "I lived with them around me all my life, but it took Ellen, a New Yorker, to realize they should be a significant part of the occasion."

Nicole felt that her outdoor wedding, held on Cape Cod, required a casual, but still elegant, invitation.

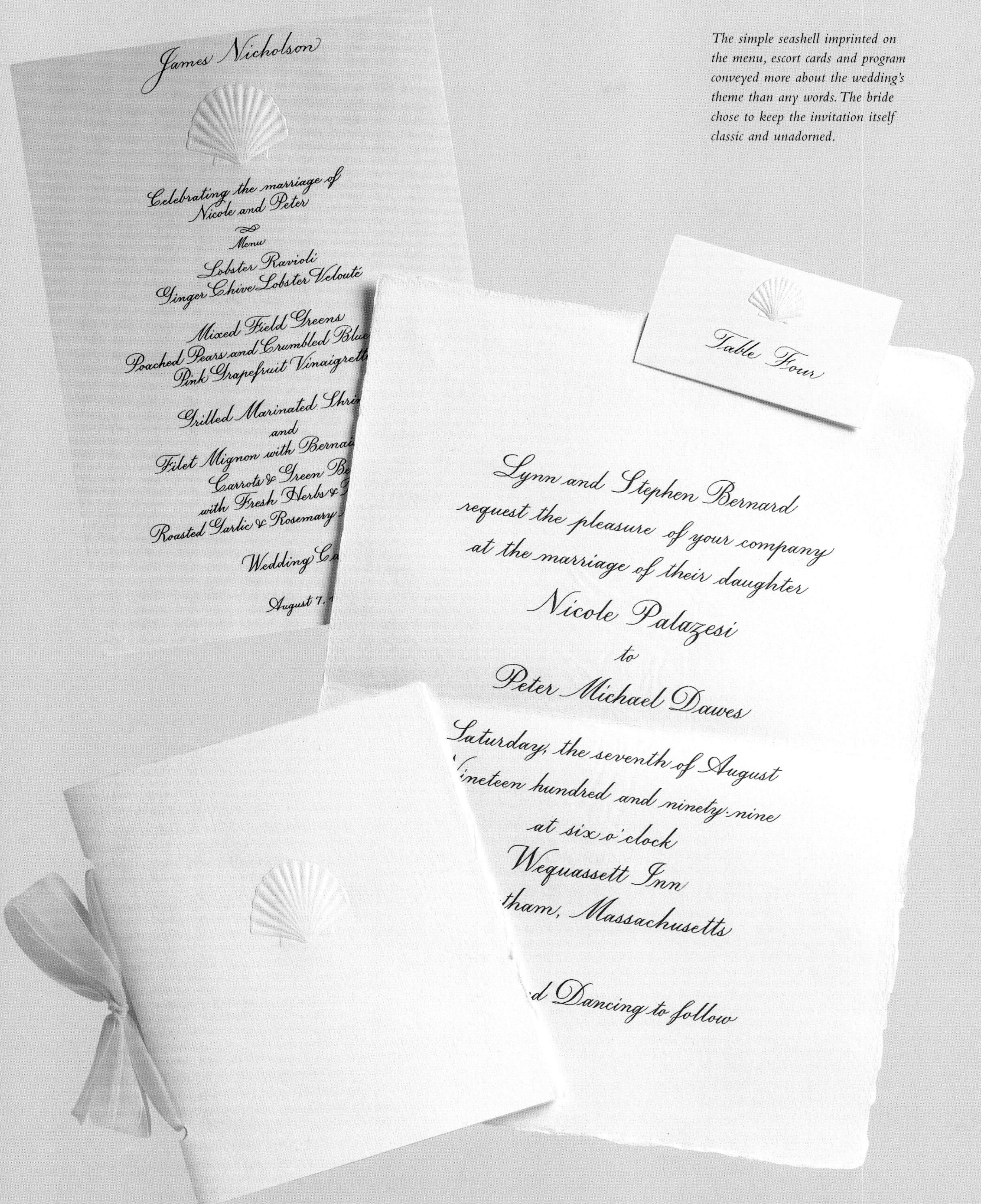

James Nicholson

Celebrating the marriage of
Nicole and Peter

Menu

Lobster Ravioli
Ginger Chive Lobster Velouté

Mixed Field Greens
Poached Pears and Crumbled Blue
Pink Grapefruit Vinaigrette

Grilled Marinated Shrimp
and
Filet Mignon with Bernaise
Carrots & Green Be
with Fresh Herbs &
Roasted Garlic & Rosemary

Wedding Ca

August 7, 1

The simple seashell imprinted on the menu, escort cards and program conveyed more about the wedding's theme than any words. The bride chose to keep the invitation itself classic and unadorned.

Table Four

Lynn and Stephen Bernard
request the pleasure of your company
at the marriage of their daughter

Nicole Palazesi

to

Peter Michael Dawes

Saturday, the seventh of August
Nineteen hundred and ninety-nine

at six o'clock

Wequassett Inn

tham, Massachusetts

d Dancing to follow

Summer Tompkins Walker's festive bevy of bridesmaids provided a crescendo of color at her 600-guest wedding on Treasure Island in San Francisco Bay.

Chapter 6
WEDDING
FASHION

*The only rule that applies when a
bride chooses a wedding gown is
that she must fall in love with it.*

Dressing in Style

"WHEN A BRIDE TRIES on the right dress she should feel confident, beautiful, elegant and, most of all, extraordinarily happy. When I designed a wedding gown for Caroline Kennedy Schlossberg, she initially told me she wanted something untraditional, maybe asymmetrical. I took the liberty of convincing her differently. We made her an organza dress—the fine, transparent material, I thought, was quite right for Hyannisport—with shamrocks appliquéd to the bodice, stitched inside the full skirt and sprinkled on the veil. Shamrocks were her father's favorite flower; she thought they would make her feel close to him on her wedding day. It was the right dress for Caroline. You know how I know? She was extraordinarily happy when she put it on."

CAROLINA HERRERA, *fashion designer*

BRIDES DELIGHT IN telling the story of the search for their wedding dress. Most portray the pursuit in a romantic fashion, as if they were describing their dating years, culminating in that certain moment when they knew they had found the Right One. Much like Caroline Kennedy, they recall feeling ecstatic when, after trying on countless gowns, they looked in the mirror and realized that they had just donned the dress of their dreams. The experience simply cannot be equated with mere shopping. After all, on the most important day of her life, a woman should be wearing the most important dress of her life.

Perhaps that is what makes choosing a wedding dress so compelling. Finding the perfect design is usually a once-in-a-lifetime event—one that many women have been dreaming about ever since childhood. The gown often assumes an other-worldly character, rather like a theater costume. "It's not something you wear in real life," says Monica Hickey, a fashion expert and bridal designer who has helped dress such discriminating brides as Amanda Burden, the Ford daughters, and Connie Chung. Even if you choose a crisp white suit, it is going to be your wedding suit and will take on a life and a meaning of its own.

So it's not surprising that the modern bride is encouraged to realize some of her own fashion fantasies through her wedding dress. Religious, family and ethnic customs all shape bridal style to some extent, but the strongest influence is undoubtedly fashion itself. Reflecting prevailing silhouettes and hem lengths, wedding-dress designs have always closely followed the styles of the times. After the lean war years of the forties, such esteemed bridal houses as Priscilla of Boston brought back the grand ballroom dress in the 1950s and made feminine A-line designs fashionable as well. Both styles remain popular today—in modern translations, of course. Bill Blass recalls creating a "wedding mini" for a Palm Beach bride in the 1960s, when skirts were worn way above the knee. ("The monsignor did raise his eyebrow a bit," the designer admits.) And who can forget Princess Diana in her twenty-five-foot train? Women all over the world clamored for copies. In the eighties, dress styles went completely over the top, with an abundance of pomp, pouf and circumstance. Another icon of style, the late Carolyn Bessette Kennedy, set the next trend. After this slim blonde donned a

"Bridal style, like all fashion, evolves with the society it is serving. It reflects the changes and yet also pays homage to the past."
—MONICA HICKEY, *Custom Bridal Couture, Saks Fifth Avenue*

white slip gown designed by Narciso Rodriguez for her 1996 wedding to John F. Kennedy, Jr., more than a few brides-to-be reassessed their own dresses with an eye to paring them down to the same nonchalant simplicity.

Simplicity remains the recurring theme. To be sure, some of the grandeur has returned to bridal design. (Not everyone can carry off a sexy sheath.) Brides still desire the royal treatment, but they are not necessarily interested in wearing the crown jewels sewn onto their bodices. Today's princess doesn't want you to know how much her kingdom is worth. Wedding fashion is now about the quality of the dress; more often than not, a look of sophisticated understatement belies the hundreds of hours of work actually put into the design and fabrication. Now, the drama might come from a single row of perfectly placed satin buttons or from the way the slimmest of pearl-studded spaghetti straps cross and recross a bare back. And as styles become more imaginative, brides are asking for strapless dresses (unheard of in years past), risking raised eyebrows with a plunging back or breaking tradition with a white Armani pantsuit.

The options are all the more exciting now that high-profile names like Bill Blass, Carolina Herrera, Badgley Mischka, Donald Deal and Angel Sanchez are offering ready-to-wear bridal collections, lending wedding-dress design a dash of their own unique—and not always traditional—flair. As you would expect, bridal gowns by these fashion greats are elegant, au courant and utterly delicious. The same can be said of those by Vera Wang, whose bridal palace on Manhattan's Madison Avenue is a regular stop on the wedding-gown circuit. A very modern blend of sultry and sweet has made this designer's name synonymous with the phrase *wedding dress* for movie stars, society women and anyone else who simply must have a "Vera." For high-style tradition, brides might consider a gown by Ulla-Maija, Richard Glasgow, Amsale Aberra or Pat Kerr, all classic designers whose dresses tend to be more typically bridal (read "princess-like"). And finally, there is couture. Such designers as Oscar de la Renta will sometimes create custom gowns for special clients, offering those lucky brides the chance to design the dress of their dreams with one of the true masters of the fashion world.

Ulla-Maija's heavy satin gown (above) is simple yet sumptuous because of the quality of the fabric.

*"Sometimes I'll bring out the exact opposite of what
a bride has been describing, and it's amazing to see her fall in love
with it. She won't take it off and she ends up buying it."*
—PAT KERR, *Memphis bridal designer*

Settling Down... with the Right Dress

SOME WOMEN KNOW exactly what they want and where they want to get it. Consider the New York bride, for instance, whose fantasy wedding gown came straight out of Jean-Honoré Fragonard's rococo painting personifying the four stages of love, which she saw at the Frick Museum. For this young woman, no mere dressmaker would do: A professional costume designer replicated the romantic creation, which featured a ruffled bustier and full skirt. "It was a princess style, but very décolleté," she recalls, "just what I was looking for."

Most brides aren't so decisive. Therefore before even setting foot in a bridal atelier, you should determine what image you want to project. The wedding dress has everything to do with the rest of the wedding: The bride sets the tone. Before you make the necessary appointments for dress showings, look through magazines to get a sense of what is out there. Consider the styles and features that already make you comfortable. High neck or off-the-shoulder? Sleeves or sleeveless? Drop-waist or fitted? A-line or full? Take a look in your closet at your favorite dresses for both day and evening and assess what you love about them. Then look for the same qualities and details in a wedding gown. Think about the fabrics and sleeve lengths that might be right for the time of day and the setting of your wedding. And don't forget practical considerations—how you are going to get a ten-foot train up an outdoor stairway in February or whether the style requires uncomfortable lingerie. Because some places of worship require women to cover their shoulders or heads, religious restrictions may also affect your choice.

Dresses can be found everywhere, from small boutiques and designer ateliers to the bridal departments of large retail stores—not to mention couture auctions, shops specializing in antique lace (or your mother's or grandmothers' attics—see "Celebrating the Past," page 103). When you start shopping, visit different types of stores and salons so that you can get used to the way dresses are shown, how designers work and the way the staff treats you. Any good salesperson or designer has a stock list of questions to ask a bride to determine how she pictures herself on her wedding day. Most couturiers use sketches, often drawing while they sit and talk to a client; Carolina Herrera will also bring out some ready-made gowns for a bride to try on to get a sense of the style she likes most. Other advice from the experts:

● Start early—at least six months before the wedding. There are two seasons for dresses: Spring/summer

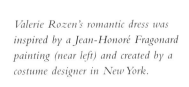

Valerie Rozen's romantic dress was inspired by a Jean-Honoré Fragonard painting (near left) and created by a costume designer in New York.

Celebrating the Past

"THE FAMILY CONNECTION was really important to me," says Ellen McNamara, a New York bride who was married in her mother's 1956 white satin wedding dress—fifteen years after her older sister wore it at her own wedding. "Wearing her dress made our mother so happy," she explains. "It was such a beautiful dress; I didn't even bother going shopping for a new one." Ellen McNamara was one of the lucky ones. Cleaned and boxed, the forty-one-year-old dress had survived beautifully. Although oxidation had caused the white satin to change color, both sisters liked the champagne hue it had turned. The only problems were a few brown age spots on the train, which an adroit seamstress was able to remove by replacing the panels with matching fabric.

Unlike Ellen McNamara, *Town & Country* Editor-in-Chief Pamela Fiori did go shopping for a new dress to wear at her wedding to advertising executive Colt Givner, but had reservations about the one she bought as the date approached. "It was made of lace and it just didn't seem like me," recalls Fiori, whose mother finally urged her to wear the beautiful dress her aunt (and godmother) had worn in the early 1950s. Of off-white satin with long sleeves, a lace bodice and a scalloped neckline, the gown—which

Town & Country *editor-in-chief Pamela Fiori proudly wore something borrowed—and subsequently lent it to another bride.*

Fiori had tried on as a little girl—was in great shape. Three or four fittings later, Fiori had her dream dress. "My aunt actually arrived late, so she didn't see me walking down the aisle," Fiori relates. "But she was behind me as I walked up the aisle, sobbing the whole way."

For brides across the country, wearing an heirloom gown provides the perfect opportunity to honor such family connections and to be married in a dress that has a history. And gowns that are handed down are hardly hand-me-downs. Older

dresses can display exquisite workmanship; in fact, the quality and value of many are so high that some auction houses, including William Doyle Galleries in New York, offer bridal gowns at special couture and wedding sales.

Stains and other blemishes often come with age, but if a particular dress is your heart's desire, don't give up. A talented conservator can fix almost any dress, no matter how old or damaged (for a price, of course). Even when there are no flaws, an heirloom dress almost always needs alteration, particularly in an era when health-club workouts have made body types significantly more muscular than a generation ago. That provides an interesting construction question, says Gina Bianco, a New York textile expert who sometimes resorts to making an entirely new dress from an heirloom that simply doesn't fit. The fabric and the nostalgia remain, but the remade dress suits the new bride's figure. "After all," says Bianco, "you don't want to be walking down the aisle looking like Kodachrome film in a period movie."

And don't forget the next generation. Gina Bianco advises packing your dress, whether old or new, in acid-free tissue and boxes. Store it in a dark, dry place to preserve it for the daughters and granddaughters of the future.

styles usually ship to the stores the previous October; dresses for the fall/winter arrive in March. A bride working with a couturier or dressmaker may need to begin shopping sooner because a custom-designed dress requires more fittings. Bridal salons, whether independent or located in a large department store, typically work by appointment only. Make one as soon as possible.

● Be open-minded. Even if you have a predetermined idea, don't let it overpower you. Try on a variety of dresses at the places that suit your shopping style best.

Overleaf: Lillian Wang wanted her Bill Blass couture gown to have many of the features she loved in her everyday clothing, such as a boat neck, high-quality fabric and an A-line shape.

The bride should wear the dress—never the other way around.

● Consider carefully whom you take along on your shopping expeditions. A wedding gown is a very difficult purchase. You want to please your mother; you want to please the groom (on the wedding day, of course). First and foremost, though, you should please yourself. Shopping for a bridal gown is a wonderful mother-daughter experience. But many designers and seasoned salespeople recommend that the bride go it alone, at least at first.

● Have enough fittings. There should be at least two— more if your gown is custom-designed or if you plan to lose weight. Make sure the final fitting is scheduled as close to the wedding as possible; brides naturally shed weight a few weeks before the big day. Wear the right lingerie. Lift your arms. Make sure you can hug people and dance. The dress should never wear the bride; it should always be the other way around.

● Check the length. Many brides end up stepping on their hems. For a full-length dress, the designer Ulla-Maija recommends a hem that falls two inches above the shoe top. Other hem styles, including tea- and knee-length, should also be checked with your bridal shoes to make sure the look is right; a higher heel makes the hem fall higher. Try your shoes on with your dress and spend some time walking around during the fittings.

● Don't obsess. Don't worry about that one flower at the shoulder or waist that doesn't seem quite right. Details can be worked out later. The most important element to decide first is the silhouette of the dress and the way it makes you feel.

● Don't get frazzled. Brides usually know when they've found The Dress, but if you feel that you have been searching high and low with nothing to show for it, perhaps you've tried on too many. Take a week's break, make a list of your favorites and the features you liked about them and try those gowns on again. If you're still dressless, consider having one designed.

Most important, be yourself. Experts advise that brides shouldn't deviate too much from their normal look in terms of hair and makeup. A little drama works well, but the dress should also look natural.

Dressing Up the Dress

ACCESSORIES ARE IMPORTANT personal touches. But beware: They can make or break the dress. The right accent—drop earrings, perhaps, or beaded mules—will only enhance a lovely bridal gown. But too much accessorizing can ruin the image.

The Romantic Reprise

THE ONLY REQUISITE in choosing the attire for a second wedding should be that the clothing and jewelry recall nothing from the first. Fashion designer Carolina Herrera wore a short, pale yellow dress of her own design—organza with piqué flowers—for her second time around. A sophisticated suit or a gown in a stunning color are also possibilities. The second-time bride can even carry off a traditional bridal gown and veil if she's having a gala wedding, as Barbra Streisand did when she married James Brolin in an ensemble designed by her best friend, Donna Karan. As for the third-time bride? "Anything goes," says Herrera.

Veils and Other Headpieces: Be it satin ribbons, a veil of layered tulle or a silk headband, bridal head wear should suit your dress in style and mood without overwhelming it, you—or your hair. Designer Amsale Aberra always advises a bride to focus first on her hairstyle. "You don't want to distort the way your hair looks," she emphasizes. A French twist may call for nothing more than an antique hair clip perfectly positioned to set off a gorgeous long neck. A tiara, which can be a regal complement to a formal dress, makes a sleek hairstyle dazzle (see Chapter 7). Silk or fresh flowers attached to a headband offer chic simplicity.

There is no question, though, that the ultimate accessory is the veil. Nothing says "bride" or adds to her mystery more eloquently. Designers typically offer several veils to go with their dresses, so you will find a range to choose from when you go shopping for your dress. Heirloom veils, which can be refashioned to work with a newer wedding gown if necessary, are another possibility. Although there are myriad styles and shapes, the primary decision involves length. A shoulder-length veil works best when the dress back features beautiful detailing that shouldn't be covered. A cathedral veil, which might be as long as ten feet, can be the dramatic complement for a formal gown. Veils with blushers designed to cover the face during the ceremony are considered the most romantic. They also provide a personal moment for the bride and her father as he briefly lifts the blusher, according to tradition, in order to gaze into his daughter's eyes after they've walked down the aisle. If you wish to wear a veil throughout the entire wedding, as tradition also dictates, you'll need to choose a length and style suited to dancing. Some brides want to keep looking like a bride all evening long rather than "the girl in the white dress," says Ulla-Maija. But others don't want to be encumbered by the veil when they're dancing. The compromise: Wear the veil for the cocktail hour and remove it just before the grand entrance to the ballroom.

Footwear: Today's bride might wear anything from white cowboy boots to white mules or sandals. Some of the newer styles feature ankle straps, t-straps, sling backs, chunky stacked heels and low Sabrina heels. Because comfort is the most important aspect, stick to what you're used to. If you usually wear heels, wear them at your wedding. If you

Jessica Friedberg chose a short veil but a long train for her walk down the aisle at New York's Rainbow Room.

wear flats, wear flats. One of the most popular styles of wedding shoe remains the proper pump with a square toe; the solid two-inch heel gives a bride support on perhaps her shakiest day ever. Another excellent standby is a simple sling back. Silk crepe and silk satin, the most fashionable shoe materials, tend to work best with most wedding-dress fabrics. Swarovski crystals can be added for sparkle.

Stylish brides are delighted that high-profile shoe designers, like dress designers, have turned their attention to bridal fashion in recent years. Among the most popular are Vanessa Noel (fabulous variety), Peter Fox and Kenneth Cole (comfortable, stylish pumps) and, of course, Manolo Blahnik (fancy and elegant). Other hot names in the wedding business include Jimmy Choo, Marc Jacobs and Sergio Rossi. Whatever the choice, try the shoes around the house for a couple of weeks. Footwear can be a pretty focal point, but most important, shoes shouldn't hurt. A bride should float through her day. With the right shoes (and, of course, with the right man), she will.

Gloves: Gloves drift in and out of style for weddings. Choosing to wear them depends on the bride, her dress and the mood she wants to set. "I'm a glove person," says Ulla-Maija. "I put gloves on everyone. When you're walking down the aisle, it looks so nice and formal." Glove designer Francesca Portolano suggests a long style in white kid for the newer sleeveless gowns, although brides may opt for

cotton or satin during the warmer months. The eternal problem with gloves is when to take them off. Portolano suggests wearing them to the church, but removing them before walking down the aisle. "In Italy, where I come from, removing your gloves at the altar is like a striptease. It's not sacred; it's not appropriate," she says. But Ulla-Maija recommends that the bride simply unbutton the fingers and fold them back when it's time to put on the ring. For this purpose, bridal gloves always have buttons near the

Long white gloves harken back to a time when gloves equaled glamour at weddings in both the United States and Europe. For many brides, gloves have always remained a must.

fingers. Don't even think about buying long gloves without buttons. Removing them would take too long during the ceremony, especially for a nervous bride with sweaty palms.

Handbags: Bridal bags are exquisitely beautiful, but generally cumbersome. A bride has so many people to kiss and hug and so much dancing to do—why does she need to lug around a pocketbook? Still, with the array of gorgeous bags available—Badgley Mischka will even design one to match a wedding gown—many women are tempted to carry one. Judith Leiber, the doyenne of evening-bag designers, has fashioned bags to look like small books, making it quite appropriate for a bride to walk down the aisle holding one. If nothing else, a bag serves as a carryall for a lipstick and handkerchief that can sit on the bride's table and look pretty. It's more of a keepsake than a useful accessory. But why shouldn't the bride have it?

In addition to these standard accessories, there are other ways to personalize your bridal wardrobe. When photographer Jill Krementz married writer Kurt Vonnegut in 1979, Monica Hickey designed a matching white bow for Krementz's Manchester terrier to wear on its head. The dog was her maid of honor. And that's fine, says Hickey, because it was the bride's personal statement of style.

Known for a more subtle approach, Pat Kerr often incorporates lace from an heirloom gown into a dress she is designing. She also receives frequent requests for styles that emphasize the dress's neckline because so many brides want to show off a special necklace. For her own personal expression, Caroline Kennedy had her embroidered shamrocks; another Herrera bride who loves butterflies asked for Chantilly lace woven with a butterfly pattern. Instead of a veil, she wore handmade organza butterflies in her hair. At the end of the ceremony, the guests opened small nets at the designated moment, and hundreds of live butterflies fluttered into the air to complete the theme.

Another bride, who works as a fashion director for a New York magazine, satisfied her lifelong passion for the designs of Coco Chanel by wearing a Chanel jacket over her Vera Wang dress. The very fitted pink-and-white blazer featured just a little sparkle. It was the ideal cover-up for her backless dress while she was in the church and gave her an extra fashion surprise to reveal during the reception. The Chanel salon also created the bride's headpiece, which incorporated a headband adorned with the designer's signature camellias and a short birdcage veil in pale pink. "The entire ensemble was entirely me," says the bride, "and it made me very happy." As every good wedding dress should.

This jeweled minaudière (above) designed by Judith Leiber is beautiful enough to be carried down the aisle.

Bridesmaids Revisited

THE POOR BRIDESMAID. She rarely gets to choose her own dress or, for that matter, the color. Typically, she has to pay for it—even if it's chartreuse. And let's not even get started analyzing that phrase "Always a bridesmaid, never a bride . . . ."

Fortunately for all concerned, the image of the bridesmaid is rapidly changing. Bridesmaids' dresses were once relegated to the back rooms of bridal boutiques, but in recent years they have taken a turn for the better, in part because ready-to-wear collections and couture are now available for the bridal party, too. Suitable for any elegant evening affair, Vera Wang's bridesmaids' dresses can actually be worn again— a remarkable feat for this category of clothing.

The ideal bridesmaid's dress is photo-friendly. Off-the-shoulder dresses can literally slide right off the shoulder, which is a look you certainly don't want immortalized in your wedding pictures. Styles should be bra-friendly and classic. Bridesmaids shouldn't look too fashion-forward; they should blend in, not stand out. The exceptions are the maid and matron of honor, whose dresses can have a distinguishing twist: a different cut in the same color as the dresses of the other women, or perhaps a matching chiffon wrap to drape over bare shoulders.

Color choice is entirely up to the bride and usually relates to a season or theme. Red or burgundy velvet is luxe for a winter wedding; pastels look fresh in summer. Although white was once verboten, the elegant, put-together look of an all-white wedding has brought white bridesmaids' dresses into fashion. Black goes in and out of style; it is not considered the most festive of colors, yet it is chic and looks good on virtually anyone. Another effective way to dress different shapes is to choose a dress that

Barefoot and bridal: This bride posed with her bridesmaids (above) shortly before her ceremony. (They put on their shoes before they walked down the aisle.)

Fashion designer Cynthia Rowley (opposite) designed her own gown, as well as those of her bridesmaids.

The mother of the bride shouldn't outshine the bride, but should look beautiful and elegant; after all, she is usually the hostess. Right, Mrs. Leonard P. Sasso and daughter Josephine share a moment alone.

comes in a few style variations, permitting the women to wear dresses in the same fabric, but in cuts that best fit their figures. A happy and comfortable bridesmaid will exude more confidence as she walks down the aisle.

What's a Mother to Wear?

IT MAY WELL BE the most difficult dress purchase of a woman's life. And it's not the bridal gown. The mother of the bride has a very fine line to walk. She shouldn't outshine the bride but obviously wants to look beautiful herself. The primary rule: A mother of the bride shouldn't wear white unless the bride specifically requests it. Ruffles, a loud color, flashy beads or other attention-getting features are appropriate only if the bride doesn't mind. Most mothers of the bride (and groom) find that classic cuts and simple detailing work best. One well-dressed mother of the bride recently found a dress by the designer and couturier John Anthony—a long strapless style in

The mother of the bride shouldn't outshine the bride, but should look beautiful and elegant; after all, she is usually the hostess. Right, Mrs. Leonard P. Sasso and daughter Josephine share a moment alone.

pale daffodil with two flowers in front and a bolero jacket for the church. Stylish and understated, it was perfect for a spring wedding replete with peonies and apple blossoms.

John Anthony, for one, takes umbrage at the term "mother-of-the-bride dress." There is no such thing, he declares. The bride is the bride. The mother of the

bride is the hostess. And she has to look absolutely wonderful because she's the one greeting guests. Carolina Herrera would agree. "The mother should be glamorous, not dowdy, and wear the best color for her," the designer says. When she was married, Caroline Kennedy recalls, Jackie was absolutely against wearing anything that bespoke "mother of the bride." She chose a beautiful silk dress in celadon. And of course, she looked absolutely amazing.

Are there different guidelines for the mother of the bride and the mother of the groom? Technically no, although the mother of the bride is traditionally considered slightly more important than the latter. The first rule is that the two women absolutely must confer. Los Angeles wedding consultant Frankie Berger recalls a wedding where both mothers wore the same dress—an especially horrible coincidence because one woman was slim and the other was quite heavy. As for accessories, Berger

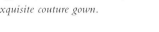

Eliza Reed worked closely with her stepfather, Oscar de la Renta, on her exquisite couture gown.

believes the essential items for both mothers are pretty handkerchiefs to match their dresses. "Without a doubt," she says, "they will both cry."

The Pint-Size Wedding Party

YOU CAN RARELY COUNT on children's behavior at weddings, but you can almost always count on their charm. Like the rest of the bridal party, the youngest members should wear clothing that complements the bridal gown in both spirit and color. Clothes should be simple and suitable to the child's age. And if children say they're uncomfortable, listen. Otherwise, you'll have a frowning child in the pictures and an uncooperative one during the ceremony and reception.

For flower girls, Julie Roshkow of Miss Pym, a fine dressmaker for girls size 2 to 14, suggests fabrics like silk organza or duchess satin—such as the bride herself might choose. Younger girls are happiest if they are given a choice of two dresses. Picking one makes them feel part of the plan, and they usually want to please the bride. After about age ten, girls tend to look too grown-up to be flower girls, but they don't have to be excluded from the wedding party. The next step is the junior bridesmaid, who should dress in a suitable version of what the older bridesmaids are wearing. Boys need not wear miniature tuxedos. "They often look like little clowns," says Pat Kerr, who prefers to see them in knickers (velvet for winter, cotton piqué for summer). Julie Roshkow sends boys to Brooks Brothers or Ralph Lauren for crisp shirts and long trousers with suspenders. She recommends seersucker suits for summer and gray flannel pants with blue blazers for winter.

Overleaf: For their wedding, Billy and Vanessa Getty eschewed typical flower girls, opting instead for flower "fairies." These three angelic girls took guests' breath away as they floated down the aisle.

Men of all ages (left and below) should allow themselves plenty of time to get dressed. Tying bow ties (especially for first-timers) can be time-consuming.

Of course, with such adorable, well-dressed kids in attendance, the bride should be prepared for a cherubic child to steal the show. When a flower girl charms the crowd by skipping down the aisle, she's going to be remembered in this role for eternity. If the children are a little bit older, they understand that their role is to set the scene for the bride, but brimming with so much personality and energy, they might just play to their audience—and to rave reviews. The best way to get children to behave? Rehearse, rehearse, rehearse. Start four weeks in advance. Get them excited about the event, but also let them know how serious and sacred it is. And prepare them for stage fright; sometimes they peek out at the crowd before they go down the aisle and freeze. Finally, know when to send the child home. Well-behaved children are

Men of all ages (left and below) should allow themselves plenty of time to get dressed. Tying bow ties (especially for first-timers) can be time-consuming.

adorable in the ceremony and welcome at the cocktail hour—and are ideally in bed asleep by the time dinner rolls around.

The Forgotten Groom (and Groomsmen)

THERE IS A REASON so little is said about the groom's attire: There isn't much to say. At a traditional black-tie dinner wedding, a groom should wear a traditional black tuxedo. White tie and tails or a morning coat is appropriate only for the most formal weddings. A black velvet dinner jacket is an acceptable alternative for a man who wants to deviate slightly from custom and project a sharper image. Other styles, like the newer collarless tuxedo dress shirts (the sort that turn up at Oscar ceremonies)

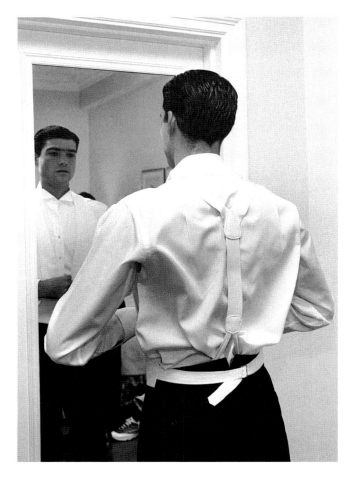

may be a breach of etiquette. For many, the lack of a tie shows a lack of respect for the occasion.

The choices broaden when the dinner isn't formal or the wedding is held at another time of day. In this case, the groom might wear a navy blazer with linen or khaki trousers or a dashing suit (Armani, Brioni or Kitano, perhaps) paired with a striking but conservative tie (in a tightly woven pattern of the sort that makes Charvet so popular). A military groom might don his dress whites for day or night. But truth be told, when the wedding is held before five o'clock and the reception is outdoors, there aren't many rules of etiquette to break. Wilkes Bashford of the venerable San Francisco clothier bearing his name has dressed grooms for innumerable afternoon weddings in the California wine country.

At the Sonoma wedding of Kira and Gordon Gould (above), the groomsmen took their fashion cue from the groom.

Etiquette

Today's brides and grooms are making some unusual choices when it comes to their wedding parties: Asking the people who are closest to them to be in their wedding often means calling on friends of the opposite sex. Some brides eschew tradition to name a close male friend as a "bridesmaid" or "maid of honor." You can bet these fellows are not wearing gowns in any shape or form, but rather boutonnieres to match the color of the female bridesmaids' dresses. Some couples do away with the bridal party altogether, asking family and close friends to participate in the ceremony instead. The bottom line is that a wedding is an occasion for closeness and warmth. Choosing the people who mean the most to you is more important than selecting those who are the right gender. As for the Goldman Sachs investment banker who walked down the aisle to the altar with his dog? These days, it seems, man's best friend can also be man's best man.

His preference is a cream-colored jacket chosen to match the bride's gown—perhaps in ivory linen. The groom's clothes, he says, should always be determined by what the bride is wearing. For this reason, most women make the decisions and tell the men how to dress.

The groomsmen's attire takes its direction from what the groom wears. If he dons a tuxedo, the ushers follow suit. If the groom wears a handsome silk jacket, the groomsmen might wear linen jackets in the same color. Groomsmen's clothes should also complement the bridesmaids' attire. If the women are dressed in silver gowns, for instance, the men could wear matching ties. The most important consideration? Good grooming. The men should look as perfect and impeccable as the women.

The newlyweds with the bride's stunning mother, actress and dancer Josephine Premice.

Wedding Style: Garden Gala

"A WEDDING DRESS is a lot like a man," says Susan Fales-Hill, a New York–based television writer and producer who was married to investment banker Aaron Hill at Grace Church in Manhattan, with a reception following at the New York Botanical Garden. "You just know." So it's not surprising that Fales-Hill felt rather unsettled when she realized she was torn between two Vera Wang dresses, both beautiful, but both lacking, well, something she just couldn't put into words. "I wanted to commit without any hesitation," she recalls. "I had been planning my wedding before I should have even dared to, so I had a vision in my head," she adds. Fales-Hill knew she wanted something very much like the Jacques Fath ballgowns that her mother had worn in the fifties, made of duchess satin with a fitted bodice and a crinoline skirt. ("Such elegance!") After many afternoons of prowling elsewhere,

Susan Fales-Hill asked her bridesmaids to choose their own black dresses because "black makes every woman look glamorous," she says.

she finally returned to Vera Wang's Madison Avenue atelier to take another look at the two original dresses. That's when a third caught her eye. "I tried it on and all the salespeople stopped what they were doing and just stared at me. At the same time, my mother walked in, took one look and said, 'That's your wedding dress, dear.' It was one of those moments you dream about." Like her mother's ballgowns of old, the Vera Wang dress was also of duchess satin. A full skirt gave the design a nostalgic ballgown silhouette while an illusion neckline created the feeling of a strapless gown without being too revealing.

So in love with the gown was Fales-Hill that she chose not to add many accessories. She wore simple Manolo Blahnik heels ("pretty high, because my husband is so tall"), a floor-length veil and little jewelry (pearl earrings and her engagement ring). Maintaining the look of simple elegance, the men wore classic tuxedos, and each of the nine bridesmaids chose her own floor-length dress in black. The bride's mother, the actress and former dancer Josephine Premice, shimmered in a silvery gray chiffon skirt, brocade tunic and taffeta jacket all designed by Koos Vandenakker. But the five flower girls truly took the guests' breath away. Garbed in lavender dresses designed by Premice, they walked down the aisle one by one, precisely as directed by the legendary choreographer Debbie Allen, a close friend of the Fales family. "They looked like Degas ballerinas," Fales-Hill recalls. "And they didn't dare miss a step, because Debbie is a true and strict dance mistress."

The bride's mother, a true Renaissance woman, designed the delightful lavender dresses for the flower girls and junior bridesmaids (opposite).

Chapter 7
BRIDAL JEWELRY

The Glitter and the Glamour

Tiffany and Louis Dubin.

"MY PARENTS GAVE ME a delicate strand of round diamonds with matching earrings to wear at my wedding. They bought them at the Andy Warhol auction. Diamonds and brides are such a natural combination: They both sparkle. I love that necklace. I wore it constantly after my wedding, I think because I wanted to keep feeling like a bride. Now, I'm saving it for my daughter to wear at her wedding. She's three and a half, but very precocious. If I let her, she would wear it to nursery school."

TIFFANY DUBIN, *vintage style specialist*

WHETHER IT'S HANDED down or purchased new, the jewelry a bride wears at her wedding is often imbued with sentiment that transcends generations and lifetimes. What could be more precious than the jewels a bride wears on her wedding day? She can't wear her dress once the wedding is over. But she can put on her jewelry. And she can also pass it on to her daughter or her daughter-in-law and to her grandchildren. Wedding jewelry is valuable simply because of the emotion it inspires.

Traditional wedding jewelry always involves pearls or diamonds or pearls and diamonds. Because nothing should outshine the face of the bride and the soul of the girl, pearls are a perfect choice. They're very good for the complexion, and they lend a glow to the features. But let us not forget brides' other best friends: The intense shine of diamonds gives a woman a sparkle that is visible from as far back as the last pew in church.

Of course, it all starts with the engagement ring—but by the time a bride reads this book, that diamond is likely to be sparkling on her finger as she turns the pages. Wedding bands are often the more difficult choice, as brides try to determine what will look best with their engagement rings. Couples shouldn't rush into the wedding-band purchase, and they shouldn't think about buying bands immediately after choosing the bride's engagement

ring. If you take some time to get a feel for the engagement ring, then you'll have a better idea whether you want a wide or a narrow band, or even a stand-alone ring for the right hand. It is also a good idea to wait to add extra bands, such as larger diamond eternity bands, until after the first year of marriage. Save them for an anniversary. After you have gotten used to your engagement ring and your wedding band, you may find you want something entirely different from your initial idea.

Lillian Wang takes a moment to read, for the first time, the inscription from her husband inside her wedding band.

"It's magic when you have an old stone from someone else's engagement ring made into new jewelry: Something old, something tried, something true."
—RENEE LEWIS, *New York jeweler*

Many brides opt to have wedding bands designed to match their engagement rings, especially if the latter are intricate. More decorative wedding-ring designs tend to work best with round engagement solitaires set on plain bands because they balance the simplicity of the engagement setting. With a simple round stone, for instance, a bride can wear a pavé band of closely set gems. Or perhaps an ornate antique band, a popular choice that offers something different from what everyone else is wearing. Square cuts or rectangular emerald cuts tend to look best with diamond-studded wedding bands that have petite versions of the engagement stone set in a channel or a bridge setting.

Stones in pear and pointed marquise cuts are more difficult to match with wedding bands because the gems are quite complex in shape. Brides who wear such engagement rings often pair them with plain platinum or gold wedding bands and choose a more distinctive band for the other hand. Linda Dunay was completely surprised by an entire set of rings presented to her by her second husband, jewelry designer Henry Dunay. "During the ceremony, he put one band on my finger. Then another. Then another," she relates. "The grand total: twelve—so that he can say 'I love you' for every month of the year." Some of the wedding bands were accented with diamonds, some were in platinum, some in gold, and all were hand-engraved on the inside with Dunay's signature hearts. Each ring is beautiful individually, and conceived as a wearable collection, the set gives Dunay's bride the ability to change the look depending upon her mood—because she can fit only four or five of them on her ring finger at any one time.

Completing the Ensemble

EARRINGS ARE THE NEXT most important bridal jewelry after rings, and brides seldom stray from the norm when wearing them. Bridal earrings usually feature pearls, often surrounded by diamonds. The primary decision is between drops and studs, a choice that can be resolved only after hair and dress styles have been determined. In this instance you might choose a style you don't often wear in everyday life to celebrate the specialness of the occasion. So if you commonly wear studs, drop earrings might add a particularly festive touch to your bridal gown.

Opera-length pearls wrapped in several lengths create an unusual and stunning effect.

When it comes to wedding jewelry, it's often best to let one piece—and one piece only—make a statement, as with this diamond choker.

that looks like too much. I prefer to see something more delicate." Camilla Bergeron has helped many brides in search of the perfect wedding necklace. A frequent request is a dog-collar choker, typically of pearls and diamonds, which works well with almost any neckline and shows off a sensuous expanse of skin between necklace and dress. But it is cutting-edge jewelry designer Renee Lewis, of New York, who makes the quintessential bridal necklace—by taking stones from antique engagement rings and setting them on platinum chains. Nothing compares, she says, to the mystique and glamour of melding past and present in this unique way.

When it comes to jewelry for the hair, tiaras make the most dramatic statements—and the most regal. The truly extravagant designs typically date from the nineteenth century. Those from the 1920s are more delicate and quite popular now among young brides. Both types can be found set with diamonds, pearls and semi-precious gems, such as moonstones. If you are worried about impressions, however, be aware that jewelers and brides alike have mixed feelings about tiaras. According to at least one jeweler, they are ostentatious: Wearing one indicates a fairly large ego (unless, of course, you really are a princess). But Fred Leighton disagrees. As long as the rest of your jewelry works with it, the highly regarded jeweler maintains, a tiara can look quite lovely.

The necklace, the next consideration, can be as dramatic as Princess Diana's famous sapphire-and-pearl choker. Or—if you don't have access to the crown jewels—as simple as your grandmother's strand of graduated pearls. The design depends on the dress, of course. But according to Camilla Dietz Bergeron, a connoisseur of antique jewelry, it also depends on the age of the bride. "I can see an older bride wearing a substantial strand of South Sea pearls around her neck," she says. "On a younger one,

Leighton's own daughter, Mara, was married in a nineteenth-century diamond bandeau—a two-inch-wide band that she wore as a headband underneath her veil. Because she

Mara Leighton, who helps run her father's antique jewelry business, wore an antique diamond headband at her wedding.

126

didn't want her wedding jewelry to compete with her dress, the bride consulted her designer, Vera Wang, who suggested mimicking the headband pattern on the train. The headband wasn't quite a tiara, but it had the same effect when she wore it atop upswept curls, rather like a coronet. "It made me feel very much like a princess, but in a delicate sense," recalls the bride. "To me, it said wedding day." And when else but your wedding day can you wear diamonds in your hair and get away with it?

Once popular for Edwardian and Victorian brides, jeweled hair ornaments have also made a comeback. Diamond barrettes are both stunning and extravagant, because few women have occasion to wear them for events other than their weddings. The sparkle, shining under a veil, is especially eye-catching. Some brides simply pin jeweled brooches in their hair. These look gorgeous atop a chignon—Audrey Hepburn style—or behind the ear. The brooch shouldn't be oversize, but rather delicate and dainty.

Five Jewelry Rules to Live By

DELICATE AND DAINTY are good bywords. Wedding jewelry always adds the glamour quotient

Antique diamond barrettes provide an unexpected sparkle in the hair. When the veil is taken off, the barrettes remain, so that the bride's hairstyle stays intact throughout the wedding.

to a wedding dress, but it is also commonly mis-worn. Perhaps the bride has on too much. Or too little (every bride needs just a little sparkle). Or perhaps the heirloom from her mother-in-law should have been reset. The good news is that jewelry mistakes are easy to avoid if you follow these simple rules:

1. Always take your wedding jewelry to the dress fitting. A bride might dream about wearing a certain pearl necklace with her wedding dress, advises Henry Dunay, but when she sees it against the neckline, it might not look right. There is a big difference between dreams and reality.

2. Make sure the jewelry doesn't compete with your gown. According to Ward Landrigan, co-owner of the legendary Verdura, of New York and Palm Beach, jewelry is almost like the music one hears at a wedding. It should set the right tone. If the gown is ornately detailed, wearing simple pieces might be better. But if the dress is plain, some jewelry is a must.

3. Don't wear too much. If your dress has a scoop neck or sweetheart neckline, says custom jewelry designer Susan Rotenstreich, the necklace should predominate over the earrings. If the dress has a high neckline, a grander pair of earrings is in order. Wearing a strong necklace and earrings, however, would be overstatement. That is always unattractive, but especially so on a bride.

"No face cream can give a bride the glow that pearl earrings do."
—Camilla Dietz Bergeron, *New York jewelry expert*

All That Glitters: Gifts of Jewelry

THERE ARE SO many wonderful aspects to a wedding. One of the loveliest is that it is traditionally a time to shower the bride, and even the groom, with gifts. Often the most intimate are jewelry, bestowed by the most important people in a bride's life. When a woman gets married, everyone gets sentimental and wants to give her a special present. The gifts should never be anything faddish, but something enduring. Sometimes parents or in-laws will purchase a new piece of jewelry for the bride, but for the mother or mother-in-law to give her something that already has some personal significance can be more meaningful.

Here are some suggestions:

Groom to bride and vice versa. The groom typically gives the bride her engagement ring, but often will also present her with a gift of jewelry as the wedding day approaches. Pearl earrings or a delicate diamond bracelet are two traditional choices. As for the bride to the groom: A dress set, cuff links or a watch—inscribed, of course—are all de rigueur. Gifts of jewelry need not be specifically earmarked to be worn at the wedding. Camilla Bergeron once had a groom come in to buy his fiancée a ruby necklace as a present to wear to their round of engagement parties and showers.

Mother-in-law to daughter-in-law. Susan Rotenstreich relates that her in-laws gave her a diamond pendant to celebrate her marriage to their son. "I still love to wear it," she says. Some women receive pearls from their future in-laws, adds the jewelry designer. But Rotenstreich notes that it is particularly lovely when a stone already in the family can be given to the bride and set however she wishes.

Mother to daughter. Fred Leighton thinks "it's a hoot" when mothers come to his store to buy a gift for their engaged daughters. "They still think of their daughters as babies and are always looking for tiny, tiny little delicate diamond things," he says. That is not necessarily what the brides want, though. Women are getting married at a later age, Leighton points out, and they are more sophisticated than ever. Family heirlooms are probably the best gifts from mother to daughter (perhaps the necklace the younger woman has lusted after her whole life). Leighton suggests a small pair of diamond drop earrings. "They're elegant and she'll wear them forever."

Parents to groom. The most traditional gifts to the groom are, once again, dress sets, cuff links and watches. Depending upon the groom's personality, the cuff links can be whimsical, perhaps antique, and representative of his interests or hobbies. Because males are generally the more challenging gender to buy presents for, gift givers may have to look to the groom's interests for ideas. Perhaps this is the time to give him a leather desk blotter and matching accessories or a monogrammed briefcase; his favorite book in a first edition; a new set of golf clubs in a monogrammed golf bag. One Connecticut groom fondly remembers the engagement gift his father-in-law offered: a tennis court for the couple's new backyard.

Bride to bridesmaids. Many brides choose to give their bridesmaids a gift of jewelry that will work both as a keepsake from the wedding and as an accessory for the wedding day. Designer Cynthia Wolff has made tiny strands of freshwater pearls for bridal parties. These days, bridesmaids are likely to be wearing different dresses to suit their figures, she says, so the necklaces tie everything together.

Groom to Groomsmen: The tastes of men don't always run to jewelry, but they still like gifts that glitter. Among the traditional choices from groom to groomsmen are silver money clips, belt buckles and pens—engraved, of course, with their initials and perhaps the date of the wedding.

This whimsical gold-wire-and-semiprecious-stone tiara, designed by Kazuko, can also be worn as a necklace.

4. Believe in the power of one. One piece of jewelry, that is. Sometimes a single stunning piece stands better alone.

5. As is true of everything else in wedding fashion, comfort should be the most important factor in choosing jewelry. Make sure the choker isn't too tight, the earrings don't pinch after half an hour, the bracelet doesn't keep catching on your skirt. That means you should try on everything before the wedding. Take the pieces to your jeweler for alterations immediately if you even suspect a potential problem.

Breaking the Rules

RULES, OF COURSE, are meant to be ignored. Especially when it comes to fashion. Renee Lewis maintains that she loves a non-traditional design on a bride: It shows a courage of spirit. Non-traditional is often defined by size. Brides tend to think in terms of delicacy, but depending upon her frame, her dress and her personality, an oversize piece can sometimes make a strong fashion statement, claims Camilla Dietz Bergeron, who recently sold a bride-to-be an exquisite and rather stately 1920s platinum necklace with overlarge aquamarines and diamonds.

Then there's color. Cynthia Wolff, the California jewelry designer, recalls creating a strand

A bride en route to the wedding (opposite) opens a surprise gift from her beloved.

Etiquette

"Something old, something new, something borrowed, something blue." Adhering to this maxim is an age-old custom, but one that has surprisingly endured, even among today's modern brides. The challenge? Something borrowed—preferably jewelry. If someone doesn't offer to lend you a piece to wear at your wedding, how do you go about, well, borrowing one? The best approach is to write a short but sweet note to the person who has something special to lend, and also means something special to you. (The bottom line: Don't request anything intimate from someone with whom you are not intimate.) The note should read something like this:

"Dear Aunt Barbara: I've always admired your diamond bracelet and would love to wear it as 'something borrowed' on my wedding day, not only because it is beautiful, but also because it is yours. I will gratefully return it the evening of my wedding . . . ."

Flattered, the recipient of the note is unlikely to refuse and likely to be quite touched.

of black South Sea pearls for a bride to wear with her white Vera Wang gown. The bride wasn't concerned about the superstition of not wearing black to one's own wedding, and the pearls really popped out on the white dress. The look, says Wolff, was smashing.

Many designers agree that color seems to work best for warm-weather weddings. A necklace of pastel stones, such as pink tourmalines, with a white summer dress is especially pretty. But colored gemstones are most often the choice of women who are remarrying. A second-time bride usually has the courage to break with the norm because she's gone the expected route once. And she may not be dressing in white, so colored jewels will work splendidly with whatever she chooses to wear.

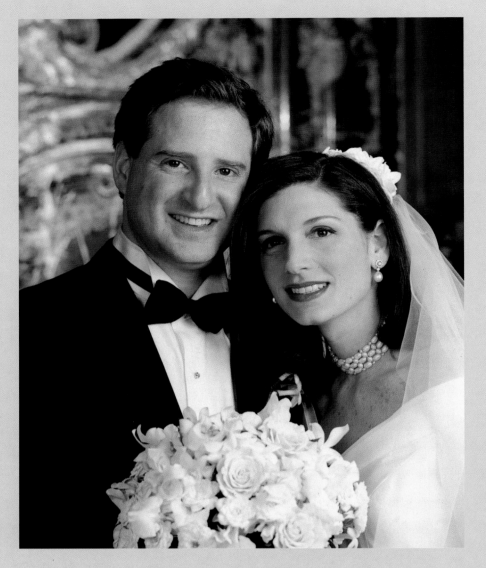

overwhelming for a woman with nowhere to wear them. So well before I found a man willing to marry me, I fantasized about walking down the aisle wearing a particular pearl choker, made by contemporary jewelry designer Gabrielle Sanchez. I love Sanchez's work because her pearls are classic in their innocence, purity and luster, but modern in their design. The choker I coveted was fashioned with Biwa pearls set in three rows designed to curve gracefully around the neck: simple, sleek and sophisticated. It was also the kind of necklace to which you can commit for life. I knew I would want to wear it time and again after my wedding.

I met Mr. Very Right. Eric proposed a year later. And then I waited for the pearls to present themselves, which they did, because I have doting parents who have always nurtured my jewelry obsession. And the dress? I wanted it to be a framework for the pearls, something completely unadorned, but made of beautiful fabric. Richard Glasgow designed the perfect creation to set off my pearl choker: an A-line dress made of duchess satin with a sweetheart neckline. Then came my earrings, South Sea pearl drops suspended from floral diamond studs, designed by the talented jewelry couturier James de Givenchy.

Wedding Style: All Choked Up

SOME GIRLS DREAM about their wedding dresses. I dreamt about my wedding jewelry. I hail from a long line of jewelry fanatics: My grandmother just happened to be named Pearl and, without question, lived up to that appellation. With her blood coursing through my veins—and a pair of her pearls swinging from my ears—I eventually became the jewelry editor of *Town & Country*, where I found that exposure to the great jewels of the world can be

Stacey Okun (above with husband, Eric Mindich) chose a simple sweetheart neckline to spotlight the contemporary pearl choker (opposite bottom) designed by Gabrielle Sanchez.

Though my husband had given me the engagement ring of my desires and a wedding band to match, I was married, according to Jewish custom, in a simple, unadorned silver band that would not detract from the true meaning of the ceremony. The ring belonged to my grandmother's sister, Rose, and my mother was married in it, too. ("something old, something borrowed.") The ten-dollar blue enamel ring that my husband spontaneously bought on the street in Venice on the day he proposed was sewn into the lining of my dress for good luck. ("something blue.") My "something new," of course, was the choker. Petite pearl drops designed by Gabrielle Sanchez were my personal gifts to my three bridesmaids. Fashioned to match my choker, the earrings worked perfectly with their simple ivory dresses.

My husband regarded the assembling of my wedding jewelry with quiet bemusement. Knowing in advance that he was marrying a jewelry aesthete, he had time to come to terms with making a commitment to a lifetime of sparkling anniversary gifts, as well as to a wife. He, however, balked at the idea of wearing a wedding ring. So we made a pact. We would buy a traditional plain gold band at Tiffany, have it engraved, and Eric would wear it at our wedding. If, after our honeymoon, he found it uncomfortable, he could put it in his drawer for safekeeping. Two children later, I'm still waiting for a complaint. But I see the pleasure he takes in wearing his wedding band and I know that it won't be forthcoming.

As for me, I still wear my wedding jewels when the occasion calls for it. Someday, I hope to be asked by a daughter or daughter-in-law to lend them as "something borrowed." Jewels are precious only if they can be handed down.

Chapter 8

THE SOUNDS
OF ROMANCE

Music to Marry By

"WHEN THEY OPENED the doors to the ballroom on the night of my wedding, the band started playing this positively ancient song, 'Yes, yes, my baby said yes, yes . . .' Everybody got the joke. And that's the way the music was for the whole night: entirely appropriate for any given moment. I wanted my wedding to seem straight out of the past, so the band used an old microphone and old instruments to capture an old sound and sang only songs from the twenties, thirties and forties. It was a freezing cold night in New York City and very still. You could hear the clip clop, clip clop, of a horse's hooves outside. Even that was beautiful music to my ears."

ANDREA MARCOVICCI, *torch singer*

NOTHING SETS THE MOOD, stirs the soul and stokes the fires of a wedding's romance better than the music. It sweetly signals the bride's entrance during the ceremony. It provides festive background for cocktail-party chatter. And during a dinner dance, the music helps the evening hit its high notes. As etiquette expert Nancy Tuckerman puts it: "Music can make or break a wedding. It should evoke a sense of who the bride and groom are, as well as entertain the guests and keep the party moving."

Though its purpose has remained the same over the years, the style and range of wedding music have changed quite considerably. It's more creative. Lately, wedding guests have seen (and heard) everything from gospel singers to solo pianists playing movie themes, such as the poignant musical motif from the film *Cinema Paradiso*. The repertoire might start with a soloist or chamber group for the ceremony, then change moods with a dance band for the reception and a deejay or jazz group for the increasingly popular post-reception party. Just as every other aspect of the modern wedding can be tailored specifically to a couple's tastes and interests, the music can also reflect their sense of formality and fun.

How to choose the best musicians? Listen to them, of course—in person. More important, talk to the bandleader. One of the most common planning mistakes a couple makes is not communicating clearly with a musician or bandleader prior to their wedding. The more input from the bride and groom about the kind of music, the timing and the feeling they want, the better their wedding will be. Couples often know they like a particular vocalist or group

because they have heard them at friends' weddings. Clubs, hotels and inns usually keep lists of the musicians who have performed successfully in their spaces, and these recommendations are also well worth looking into because the groups are already familiar with the acoustics of a location. In some instances, you may also be able to listen briefly and inconspicuously when a musician or band plays at an occasion to which you are not invited.

Other tips on selecting musicians:
● The reputation of the bandleader is very important. Be specific if you want the headliner. Many leaders have several bands within their companies but perform with only one of them. If the headliner is booked, or too expensive for your budget, make sure to meet the members of the alternate bands and listen to them play.
● Be wary of recordings. Never hire a musician on the basis of these alone; for the tape, bands sometimes use studio musicians who don't otherwise play with them regularly. The same goes for videos. They are not very representative because they are produced under simulated conditions.
● Consider the space capabilities. Location and music are important decisions to make in tandem. Outdoor settings, for instance, can be challenging because they usually require a special speaker system and access to electrical outlets. Indoors or out, make sure that the chosen musicians can fit physically in their allocated area. You might desire the sounds of a twelve-piece band, only to discover that just eight musicians will fit into the area reserved for them. In this event, you should discuss with the musicians how to achieve the sound you want without the

What kind of songs does one play for
a torch singer? At Andrea Marcovicci's
wedding to Daniel Reichert (opposite),
love songs—only love songs.

extra players, or check with the location manager to see if they can be accommodated in another spot.

● The music should also suit the space. Large rooms require large bands or small bands that are capable of producing a big sound. Similarly, small spaces will be overwhelmed by a big sound. Small bands typically have one vocalist, while larger groups feature two or three, which is another factor to keep in mind.

● Be as specific as possible. "We're happy to take lists of favorite songs," says Gene Donati, of the eponymous Washington, D.C., orchestra, which has played at the wedding of Al Gore's daughter, Karenna, and for every president since John F. Kennedy in 1961. Any reputable group should have the same attitude.

● Understand all the terms well in advance. One key factor is the overtime policy: Make sure the musicians will be available and willing to play if you suddenly decide at one in the morning that you want your wedding to last until two.

The Ceremony

TRADITION HAS ALWAYS been part and parcel of ceremony music. To this day, most brides still choose the same pieces that were played generations ago, from the bridal chorus of *Lohengrin* ("Here Comes the Bride") to the classic Hebrew composition "Erev shel Shoshanim" ("Night of the Roses").

1. "Bridal Chorus" from *Lohengrin* ("Here Comes the Bride"), Wagner
2. "Wedding March" from *Midsummer Night's Dream*, Mendelssohn
3. "Canon" in D Minor, Pachelbel
4. "Ave Maria"
5. "Ode to Joy," Beethoven
6. "Bourée" from *Water Music*, Handel
7. "The Four Seasons," Vivaldi
8. "Music for the Royal Fireworks," Handel
9. "Trumpet Fanfare," Jean-Joseph Mouret
10. "Te Deum" (ancient Catholic liturgical piece, played at Princess Diana's wedding to Prince Charles)

To create the perfect sound for the ceremony, orchestra leader Michael Carney, who plays for weddings all over the country, always suggests a string quartet, perhaps with the addition of a flute, piano or harp. The music actually begins before the service, when the customary classical compositions set the mood as guests take their seats. The processional music heralds the start of the ceremony and includes one piece to accompany the bridal party and a second, distinct piece of music for the bride. Any additional music may differ depending upon the rites. In a synagogue you might expect to hear musicians accompany the cantor or rabbi; at a church ceremony the congregation will likely sing hymns, accompanied by an organist. (Note: There is no law forcing you to use the church's own organist.) The ceremony concludes with the recessional, often a march or other celebratory piece, to accompany the wedding party's departure.

Most important, the music—be it traditional or contemporary—should reflect the couple's

"Violins are a must at a wedding ceremony. They have this quality that's capable of bringing on the tears."

—MARK STEVENS, *leader, Starlight Orchestra*

personalities and the joy of the occasion. *Today* show co-host Matt Lauer and his wife, the model Annette Roque, had a boys' choir sing them down the aisle, as well as a soloist who performed during the service. One Manhattan bride who chose Mark Stevens's traditional dance band, Starlight, for her reception wanted something light and rather untraditional for her ceremony. In fact, she actually chanted part of the "Song of Songs" in Hebrew, something very few Jewish brides do. She also chose to add a few other things that brides rarely do. "I didn't want my bridesmaids to walk down the aisle in a stiff and formal way. So we played canned music and asked them to saunter down and wave to people, blowing kisses," she recalls. Their song: "Thank Heaven for Little Girls." The bride and groom came down the aisle with their respective parents to the sound of Natalie Cole singing "Unforgettable" and returned as newlyweds to "Brown-Eyed Girl"—which, of course, the bride is.

The Reception

IT'S A TRIED-AND-TRUE format. After cocktails, bride and groom make their grand entrance to the main reception area and dance their first dance. The meal is served, and between courses the music ranges from gentle and romantic to fast and festive. A good bandleader will deliberately build the party to a crescendo, starting with slow melodies and moving along to lively dancing music after dinner is well under way.

The cocktail hour, however, is when the party begins. The perfect cocktail party music is background music, so it should be unobtrusive. Conversation, and the drinks, are the order of the hour. This is also the first chance most guests will have to greet the bride and groom and their families. That's why bandleaders suggest limiting the repertoire to jazz standards or familiar Cole Porter or George Gershwin favorites performed by a small combo.

The cocktail hour is also the ideal time for a bit of entertainment, which gives the crowd something to talk about while getting them into the spirit of the party. One frequent choice for cocktail entertainment is the Persuasions, a New York-based a cappella group specializing in love ballads. Members of this charismatic quintet might stroll around the room, singing a song now and then as background music, or they might give a single

When the orchestra takes a break, why not find a soloist from the local philharmonic to perform dinner music?

> *"There is a certain moment for spontaneous behavior and music.*
> *You can't plan it. You have to sense it."*
> —PETER DUCHIN, *leader, Peter Duchin Orchestra*

performance lasting fifteen to twenty minutes. Another popular option is a small group of strolling violinists. Both Barbra Streisand and Andrea Marcovicci had violinists play at their weddings. Marcovicci maintains that they carry the romance from the ceremony into the next phase of the wedding. And for dramatic effect, they can also escort the guests from cocktails to the wedding meal.

Nothing is more critical to the all-important flow of the party than the orchestra music. A good bandleader will feel the pulse of the room and intuitively know the right time to play certain music. "As a leader, you have to be aware of what's going on at every moment," says the renowned orchestra leader Peter Duchin. "There's a certain moment for spontaneous behavior and music," he adds. "You can't plan it. You have to sense it." A successful bandleader also incorporates a variety of styles and types of music into the mix. Much of that choice is

governed by the type of music in vogue at the time. "Dance band music completely changed after rock and roll became popular," says Duchin, who recalls that when he opened at the St. Regis Hotel in 1962, he was still playing traditional dance melodies. "When I introduced Beatles songs a few years later, people were so shocked they came over to the bandstand to express their horror. Of course, ten years after that," Duchin points out, "everyone was twisting and boogying."

Rock and roll and its subsequent incarnations have made the wedding a more dance-oriented event. And so have the ensuing fascinations with disco, jazz and swing. Unless a bride requests otherwise, the band's repertoire should consist of cheek-to-cheek music (Porter, Gershwin) intermingled with medleys of Motown, some of disco and swing (Tommy Dorsey, Glenn Miller), along with fifties rock (Elvis Presley) and Beatles standbys. Of course, some couples want the music to reflect their interests alone. At Andrea Marcovicci's wedding, the music never lapsed into rock and roll. "We wanted old-fashioned dancing only," says the bride, who ended the evening by singing "The Way You Look Tonight."

A harpist's lyrical melodies (top) welcomed guests for a ceremony held in Napa Valley. Rockola—a San Francisco band featuring music from the 60s, 70s and 80s, complete with costume changes (right)—performed at the wedding of Summer Tompkins and Brookes Walker III.

Toasting—Not Roasting

THE WEDDING TOAST is an art form that too few people get to perfect because they deliver only a couple of them in their lifetime. "The toasts should be heartfelt, articulate, witty and well practiced," says Peter Duchin. "Most important: well practiced!" And limited in number. Over-toasting can be a common problem, as wedding guests are made to listen to endless speeches when they crave dinner or a chance to run to the rest room. That said, a kind and witty, and brief, toast that will mean something to the couple and their families is always welcome.

WHO should give it: the father of the bride, as a way of greeting guests. The mother of the bride might also be invited to say a few words (especially if the parents are divorced) and occasionally the groom's parents are, too. The best man and the maid or matron of honor are also frequently asked by the couple to say a few words, although their role is better served as toastmasters for the rehearsal dinner. Finally, the groom, alone or with the bride, can offer brief thanks to the hosts, the people responsible for introducing them or to guests who came from far away.

WHAT it should include: short anecdotes, brief histories of the courtship, memories of the first time the speaker met the bride or groom and warm wishes for the future.

WHAT it should not say: anything too personal, embarrassing, crude or long-winded.

WHEN it should be given: after the first dance and before the meal is served. Some couples who plan on numerous toasts schedule them to occur at the end of each course. If the father of the bride is the only speaker, the toast can be slated for just before or after the cake cutting.

There are, of course, no hard and fast rules. And creative toasts, done in good taste, can be wonderful show-stoppers. Elliott Pollack, a well-known Hartford attorney, sang his toast to his daughter, Jessica, also a lawyer, at her Connecticut country-club wedding. Called "A Little Advice," and performed to piano accompaniment, the song chronicled the musings of an adoring father not quite ready to "give his daughter away." Starting off with the father declaring that because his daughter has now tied the knot, he mustn't meddle, he mustn't pry—it concluded with a dozen stanzas full of meddling advice. "Most wedding toasts are so typical," says the father of the bride, who, fortunately, has a fine singing voice. "I wanted to surprise my daughter and do something original." His lighthearted but emotional offering brought the house down.

The only real rule is to keep the wedding flowing. There should never be a moment when one song doesn't move into the next. Even if the band takes a break, replacement musicians or recorded music should fill the gap. The music should pause for only a few important moments: the toasts.

Good flow also means that the bandleader and the head caterer must work in tandem (see Chapter 1). This teamwork assures that guests can eat while their meals are hot and can also be distracted by marvelous music while the tables are being cleared between courses. A great reception also offers lots of surprises along the way—maybe the appearance of a well-known singer to serenade the newlyweds. Another idea is to hire a swing band to play for an hour. Limiting the time is a good idea for any kind of novelty music so that the novelty doesn't overwhelm the party.

An increasingly popular alternative to the traditional dinner dance is to postpone any serious dancing until after the cake is cut. This plan separates the dinner from the dancing, giving people a chance to talk first and pick up the pace later. Some guests can be put off by loud music when it is played too early. An elegant dinner party moving into dancing later in the evening allows everyone to have a better time. During the meal, the band should be instructed to play background music that invites people to dance quietly if they choose, but also allows for conversation.

Making the Party Your Own

THERE ARE DOZENS of ways to make a wedding intimate, no matter how long the guest list is. Music is one of the best. The closeness can start with the bride and groom's first dance. The selection of a song that has significance to the newlyweds immediately sends a message. Gene Donati recalls a couple who chose "Let's Call the Whole Thing Off" for their first dance. People loved the gesture because it created a very funny, light moment after a very moving ceremony. It was also very

much in line with the couple's personalities—as was another bride's choice of Shadrack, a blues-style jazz group whose members all wore black turtlenecks and slacks to perform at the reception, held at the rather formal New York Botanical Garden. While the musicians were able to play all the wedding standards, their stylish image mirrored the couple's own far better than a traditional dance band could have.

Yet another couple, married at the Four Seasons Biltmore in Santa Barbara, were preceded into the ballroom by twenty violinists who played "Fly Me to the Moon" while surrounding the newlyweds on the dance floor. "We felt like we were being serenaded," recalls the bride. The couple was truly serenaded at their ceremony, when Kenny Loggins walked in as a personal surprise and sang his popular ballad, "For the First Time," the bride and groom's favorite song. At Susan Fales's and Aaron Hill's reception (see pages 118–19), the guests got up to sing and dance. Of course, these guests weren't exactly unknown. Debbie Allen and George Faison turned into Fred and Ginger on the dance floor. And Chita Rivera and Lynn Whitfield also engaged in a dance-off. That joyous occasion, which united the world of entertainment (the bride's side) and the world of investment banking (the groom's), was also a meeting of two multi-cultural families with roots ranging from the Caribbean to New England.

Ten Classic Wedding Dance Songs

"THE MOST POPULAR first-dance songs are often the themes to the popular movies at the moment," says orchestra leader Michael Carney, who suggests the ten songs listed here. "But one of my favorite things about my job is to hear what choice the couple has made. You never really know what they're going to come up with."
1. "It Had to Be You"
2. "Have I Told You Lately That I Love You?"
3. "Unforgettable"
4. "The Way You Look Tonight"
5. "All I Ask of You"
6. "What a Wonderful World"
7. "As Time Goes By"
8. "Unchained Melody"
9. "You're the Best Thing That Ever Happened to Me"
10. "Always and Forever"

There are very few times in your life when the dance floor is yours and yours alone (left and opposite). Make those times count.

And that meeting took place primarily on the dance floor. "It became," concludes the bride, "a very, very personal event with many surprising, memorable moments."

After Hours

THE TRADITIONAL post-wedding party is simply an extension of the reception, when the band is paid overtime and the musicians are asked to continue playing for a few more hours. A second, popular option is to create a disco atmosphere by adding strobe lighting and hiring a deejay to play recorded dance music. For either scenario, consider serving some additional food, perhaps offering a cappuccino bar with biscotti, Stilton and fruit (see Chapter 3).

The third and most dramatic new idea is to throw a surprise after-hours night-club party. The surprise is that the "nightclub" is located in the same space as the reception—in a separate partitioned area, perhaps, or in another tent. Among the most magical examples is the temporary "Club Morocco" that florist Preston Bailey created at the St. Regis for the after-wedding party of a New York attorney. The club's

Before and after: Floral designer Preston Bailey transformed a room (above) on the roof of the St. Regis Hotel in Manhattan for a sleek all-black-and-white after-hours jazz party.

spare black-and-white decor was complete with checkerboard floor (put down right over the carpet), frosted-glass fixtures, Art Deco sofas and chairs (rented for the occasion) and lamp-lit side tables topped by vases of single calla lilies as the only floral decoration. Guests drank champagne, puffed cigars, munched on tenderloin sandwiches and talked into the night as a bass player and pianist dressed in white dinner jackets played the blues. Everyone was completely surprised because Bailey had purposely curtained off the area. It was the perfect way to extend a wedding that no one wanted to end.

Wedding planner Marcy Blum recommends making the party last with a late-night martini bar where she stocks coffee tables with magazines and boxes of cigars. She'll often engage a performance artist or other entertainment. At one of her unforgettable after parties, professional face painters airbrushed Venetian masks and extravagant jewelry onto the female guests. People who would have typically left at midnight, says Blum, stayed until 3 a.m. It was fun, it was memorable and it challenged the notion of what wedding entertainment is supposed to be about.

Etiquette

No matter how wonderful the band sounds, the music is still likely to be too loud for the guests whose table is closest to the bandstand. Of course, if the location allows, all the tables can be set back from the music, although most ballrooms and clubs don't have ample space for that luxury. So the question is: Who should sit closest to the band? The people who are most likely to be on the dance floor for the majority of the party, which typically means the youngest guests. A table full of teenagers might actually enjoy the spot closest to the band; a table of twenty-somethings probably won't notice if they're occupied with the dancing.

Guests mingled at the Gallatin Gateway Inn after the ceremony.

Wedding Style: Tradition with a Twist

SHE GREW UP LISTENING to the classic sounds of the Peter Duchin Orchestra, because the venerable and world-renowned Peter Duchin just happens to be her father. But Courtnay Duchin, a Seattle-based graphic designer, eschewed traditional wedding music at her wedding to William Kleindl. Married in Bozeman, Montana, where the couple owns a second home, they opted for a "country-western-rockabilly" band, Montana Rose. "My husband and I have very wide and diverse musical taste and we wanted something different," says the bride, who chose Gallatin Gateway, an old 1920s train depot transformed into an inn, as her setting. "It was either Montana or Africa," she says. "We really wanted space."

The band played lots of swing and country music, which had everyone dancing during the reception—even dear old Dad himself. "It was a hell of a good party," says the father of the bride, who was not at all insulted that his daughter didn't ask him to perform at her wedding. "It was outdoors, relaxed and totally informal—the perfect choice for Courtnay." But the younger Duchin didn't completely throw tradition to the wind. She and her husband danced their first dance to "Fly Me to the Moon," which Montana Rose obligingly performed in a traditional rendition. Because the bride is Jewish, the band also played its own rockabilly version of the hora. At the ceremony, she entered to a recording of Hungarian folk music from a film that she once worked on. Her father wasn't pleased with the choice, but "he wasn't so unhappy," she says, "that he didn't just love walking me down the aisle."

Courtnay and husband William Kleindl (left) sealed their commitment—as a rockabilly band played in the background. Peter Duchin and daughter (above) share a love of music—just not the same music.

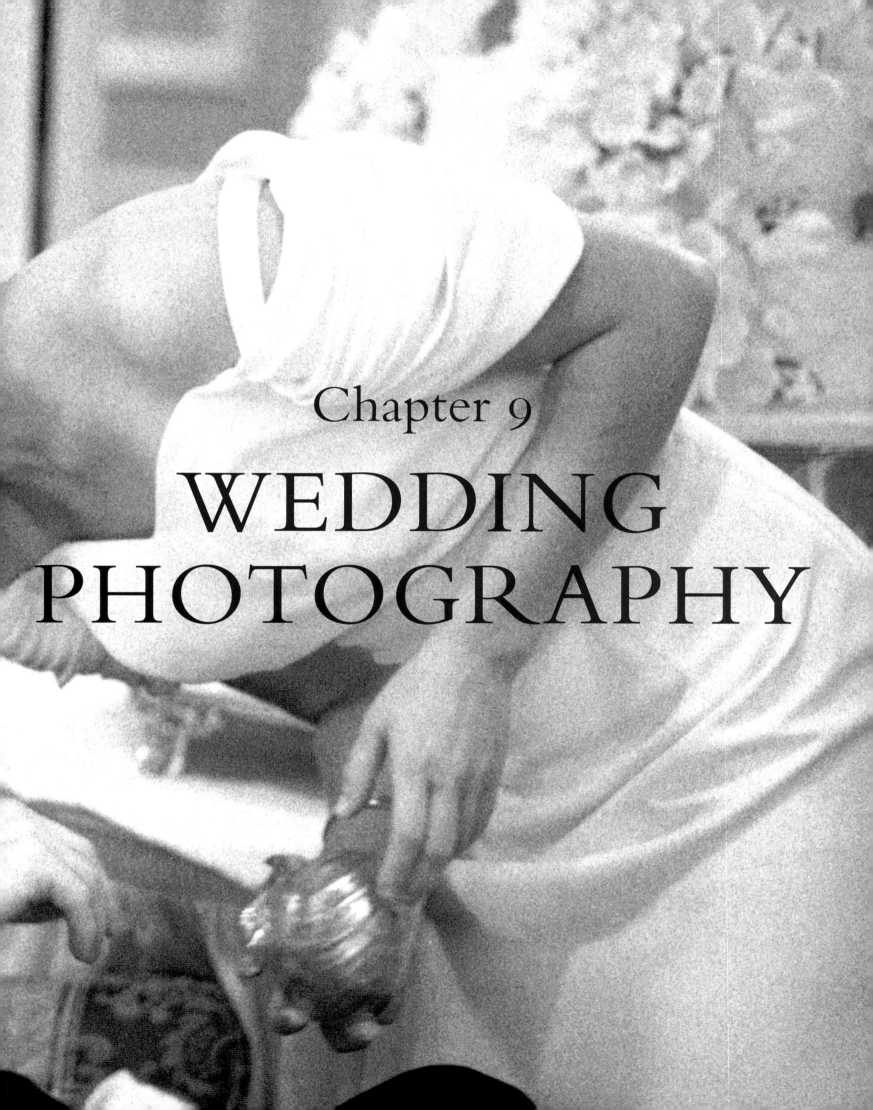

Chapter 9
WEDDING PHOTOGRAPHY

Bobbi Brown and husband, Steven Plofker.

Preserving the Memories

"I DID SOMETHING untraditional with my wedding photographs. I asked a member of the paparazzi—Roxanne Lowitt—to shoot them. She took mostly black-and-white pictures. I don't think I ever looked better in my entire life. I glowed. And there wasn't one picture of me without an enormous smile on my face. My one regret? I wish I had a professional video. At the time, wedding videos were still a new phenomenon, and I thought it would be too intrusive. My father-in-law did make a video of my wedding, but his friends are the only people in it."

BOBBI BROWN, *leading beauty expert*

"I firmly believe that people look their best when they are not aware of the camera and when small imperfections come through the lens."

—DENIS REGGIE, *Atlanta and New York wedding photographer*

THERE IS SOMETHING romantic, nostalgic and old-fashioned about wedding albums from fifty, forty, thirty, even twenty years ago. They read like a favorite fairy tale, one that you know by heart but don't mind hearing again and again. That is precisely why many couples choose to compose their wedding albums exactly the same way their parents did.

But many do not. As most wedding photographers will attest, a single word is on the lips of modern brides when describing what they want from their pictures. The word is *candid*, and it has revolutionized the way wedding photographs are taken and wedding albums designed. The fashion for pictures that capture the essence of the day in candid, documentary style means that it is now possible to preserve the memories without being bothered to pose and smile, pose and smile.

A candid style doesn't mean that your pictures can't convey the formal significance of the day. But if you want them imbued with real meaning, you need a photographer who understands how to anticipate the important events and traditions, and who can also quietly observe, sense and document the subtle moments that add texture and depth to the account. One of the leaders in this art is Denis Reggie, of Atlanta and New York, who is famed for his legendary shot of John F. Kennedy, Jr., kissing the hand of Carolyn Bessette on the steps of a tiny Georgia church. According to Reggie, capturing such compelling images means no "hold still, look here and smile" shots. No staged adjusting of veils. Instead, a really good wedding photographer employs a quick hand and a quick eye, and has the ability to preserve forever those spontaneous gestures of elation and surprise that let the couple—rather than the professional—tell their story. The photographer shoots the action—and also the reaction: a mother or grandmother watching as she remembers her own cake, or the tear rolling down a father's cheek as he gives his daughter away.

Some of the best spontaneous pictures come from what Denis Reggie calls the "transformation" stage: photos shot when the bride is getting dressed with her bridesmaids and is so concerned with the preparation that she is unaware of the camera. The idea, in other words, is to capture real moments in a real context. So be wary of the photographer who seems preoccupied with synchronizing strobes so that every

Photographer Denis Reggie caught this bride unaware as she studied herself in the mirror before the ceremony.

picture has the benefit of controlled lighting. That's a wonderful thing—if it's the look you want. Another approach is to use available light to capitalize on the warm ambiance of a candlelit ballroom and record the space as it is, not as the photographer feels it should be.

Making a Choice

THERE ARE ESSENTIALLY two types of wedding photographer: the traditionalist (a portrait photographer) and the photojournalist, (primarily a documentarian). Of course, it is possible to find someone who can combine the two approaches. But couples should be aware of the look they want when interviewing candidates. Traditional portrait photographers

often have trouble making the switch to a documentary style. Note also that photographers who specialize in other disciplines are not always the best choice for weddings. Fashion photographers, for example, are accustomed to professional models and substantial production support. Bobbi Brown had a wonderful experience with paparazzi photographer Roxanne Lowitt, possibly because Brown's long career of making up models for magazine photography has given her a more sophisticated eye than the average bride's. And unlike a magazine shoot, a wedding cannot be restaged. Choosing the wrong person to document it can result in disappointing pictures of the most important day of your life.

The best way to choose a wedding photographer is obviously to inspect his or her work, not only

Preferring to work in a documentary style, Denis Reggie is able to depict private and public moments of couples without the stiffness of a posed picture (above).

in professional portfolios, but also in the wedding albums of your friends. Photographers usually charge one fee that covers the shooting of the wedding (five or six hours), expenses, an assistant and contact sheets or preliminary prints (proofs) of the pictures, from which the final shots are chosen. The rest varies, but the fee also typically includes one album and a certain number of individual photos in wallet and/or other sizes; anything more is usually extra. That said, every photographer has his or her own way of working, so be sure you understand the fees in advance. Other advice:

● When poring through a photographer's albums, check for consistency. Make sure that the style you like in one album is repeated in others so you can be certain this photographer can do the same for you.

● Try to find a personality match. Of all the professionals involved, the photographer is the one who will be there for every minute of the wedding day. He or she should be professional and comfortable to be with and should have the same sense of appropriateness and humor as the bride and groom. A bride needs to be relaxed on her wedding day. If the photographer makes you uneasy, find someone else.

● Most photographers plan with the bride, but make sure the photographer meets the groom, too. It is just as important for the two of them to have a rapport.

● Look for flexibility. The photographer should be willing to discuss everything in detail and be amenable to all requests, or at least have alternate ideas. If there's a certain way a bride wants traditional photos such as the first dance shot, the photographer should listen and take note. Many traditional portraitists actually stage scenes when it is time to cut the cake or make the toasts, so speak up if that's not what you want. Staging photos can really interrupt the flow of the wedding and the natural behavior of the cast of characters.

● Consider hiring two professionals from the same firm to work as a tag team. "We got to see pictures of us walking down the aisle from two different angles," says a New York bride who had her hotel wedding ceremony unobtrusively covered from both front and back. "The photographers were able to capture an incredible amount without our noticing them at all," she recalls.

● And finally, think about a dry run. When a bride and groom who wed at Mar-A-Lago in Palm Beach hired Michelle Mcminn as their photographer, she insisted they all meet a few days ahead of time so that she could get to know them as

For photographer Tanya Lawson, the intimate moments reveal the true essence of a wedding.

a couple. Although they were reluctant to take the time when they were so busy, the pair consented to a casual shoot on the beach. They were so relaxed that those pictures turned out to be the best ones of all. Unbeknownst to the bride and groom, who were delighted by the gracious gesture, Mcminn enlarged a selection and mounted them on the walls of the restaurant where the rehearsal dinner took place. She also visited Mar-A-Lago several times to plan ahead.

Wedding Portraits: Before or After?

NO MATTER HOW interested they are in candid shots, most couples want portraits of their wedding party and family. Portraits are important for family history. Moreover, most extended families don't get together often, so a wedding is a time to make that happen and document it. Many photographers say that a different energy emerges when you put a group of people together. It can also be a lot of fun.

One perpetually debated question, however, is whether the portrait photography should occur before or after the ceremony. Tradition, superstition and sometimes religion dictate that the couple not see each other until the bride walks down the aisle. Practicality, however, suggests otherwise. Yes, you will miss out on that thrill of seeing each other for the first time during the ceremony with the romantic effect of background music. (How many times does that happen in your life?) But

getting the portrait shots finished—without taking time out of the reception—is too tempting for many couples to pass up.

No matter what their style, wedding photographers have passionate feelings about this debate. Denis Reggie is one who feels that photography shouldn't supersede the events of the day. And he doesn't believe brides and grooms need to see each other before the ceremony. Some photographers find that pictures of the couple taken beforehand lack the sense of excitement that occurs when the bride and groom see each other for the first time that day at their ceremony. Yet others maintain that the couple are more focused if pulled aside before the service. Later, they're too excited and have less patience for pictures.

In the end, it's a personal decision, one that the couple, not their parents, should make. A possible compromise is to take all the portraits in which the bride and groom appear apart (individual portraits, bride and bridesmaids, and the like) prior to the ceremony. Thus, only those pictures that include the couple together are left for later. The portrait photography requires at least an hour (or more for a particularly large family or wedding party), which is one obvious argument for finishing most of it beforehand. And be sure to leave at least fifteen minutes before the ceremony for the bride to return to her dressing room or another quiet place to collect herself.

Wedding portraits do have to be organized, but they

Two portraits of Mr. and Mrs. Brian Alfred Stein at their wedding: one by photographer Eliot Holtzman (opposite) and one with the photographer (right) by Mark Royce.

Overleaf: Photographer Miki Duisterhof was poised with her camera as Rory O'Connor gracefully lifted Jessica Sawyer from the carriage.

In this clearly posed shot requested by
Hamptons bride Jackie Prophit, Mallory
Samson created art in black and white.

Black and White
and Read All Over

"EVERYTHING THAT'S OLD is new again," says
New York photographer Sarah Merians about the
swing back to black-and-white wedding pictures.
Not so long ago, black-and-white pictures were
associated solely with the albums of parents and
grandparents (and they didn't have much, if any,
choice). But these days, the format is considered
glamorous by some brides—who generally have
ample color photographs taken as well. Some consider black and white a finer art than color because
it strips away most of the extraneous elements and

don't necessarily have to be formal. When Mallory
Samson, of New York and Sausalito, encountered a
group of groomsmen who were not at ease during
the portrait-taking, she asked them to stand behind a
hedge so that only their heads showed atop the
greenery. "The idea gave the guys a laugh and loos-
ened them up. It was a very comical picture," she
recalls, "but also kind of sweet." Some brides actually
request posed portraits to give their wedding albums
a deliberately antiquated look in a modern context.
Fashion stylist Jackie Prophit, who was wed at her
family residence in seaside Bridgehampton, New
York, for instance, asked Samson to arrive early so
the photographer could begin taking pictures while
the bride was getting ready the morning of the wedding. That gave Samson the opportunity to take still
lifes of the setting without any guests, and to spend
time on a few planned shots that were specifically
requested. One of the bride's favorites is a wide-
angle photo of her and her bridesmaids spread out
on the vast lawn in a very 1950s pose. Having a
chance to play, says Prophit, gave the group the
opportunity to pose for a lot of fun, old-fashioned
photographs that made the bride's album personal
and distinctive.

Photographer Holger
Thoss captured this
bride in a swirl of tulle.

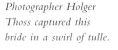

EVERY COUPLE ENDS up posing for at least a few pictures on their wedding day. But many have trouble with the key component of the photo: smiling. It's very hard to smile on cue, especially when you're anxious. So how do wedding photographers get their subjects to do it?

"I tell them to say the word *sex*," relates Toronto photographer Mark Stern. "It makes them loosen up with a more spontaneous laugh." Stern's other favorite suggestions to replace the old-fashioned *cheese*: *fuzzy peaches, fuzzy pickles, fuzzy bananas*. He doesn't know why, but these combinations of words make mouths move in a certain way, and the result is very natural. A tape of the couple's favorite music can also put them in the right frame of mind. Some photographers have the bride give her father a kiss on the cheek,

Newlyweds Michael and Valerie Rozen.
Photograph by Terry Gruber.

or tell the bride and groom to talk to each other, then capture them in the more natural moments. Others joke around with the couple and draw them out for a natural smile, then shoot quickly, paparazzi style, to get all the expressions on film.

New York photographer Julie Skarratt has her own method. "I smile at them first," she says. "People always say to me that doing the photographs was so easy because I had this great big smile on my face the whole time. Well, weddings make me happy." Besides, she adds, brides smile so much on their wedding day that they fill plenty of photographs. "As the photographer, you just have to capture it—and let the moment create itself."

focuses attention on the basics. Black and white can also be more forgiving. Julie Skarratt, a former model who is now a prominent New York wedding photographer, recalls one groom who had a professional shave a few hours before the wedding. The styptic pencil used to treat a nick got in the groom's eyes, and when he came down for the pictures, he looked as though he'd been crying for hours. What's a photographer to do? "We used a lot of black-and-white film that day," says Skarratt. "It's very good for disguising red eyes."

Black and white also creates a certain timeless air. Sarah Merians once photographed a wedding entirely in black and white, with the exception of the ceremony, which took place in a beautiful rose garden in full bloom. The service was shot entirely in color. The couple's album had a magical, *Wizard of Oz* look to it. "You expected to see the bride wearing ruby red slippers under her gown," reacalls Merians.

The New Videography

THEY HAVE TRADITIONALLY been the most despised professionals who work at weddings (disliked by the guests they put on the spot and make uncomfortable). Their cameras, and even more irksome, their bright shining lights, have made them the most noticeable, too. But videographers are much more appreciated these days. New high-tech equipment that doesn't require intrusive lighting means

"I consider myself a panther in the night. I slink around observing and shooting without getting into people's way."

—TONY ARZT, *New York videographer*

To loosen up this initially stiff group of San Francisco groomsmen, photographer Linda Russell literally got them jumping.

Julie Skarratt, a former-model-turned-wedding-photographer, captured this sparkling moment: bridesmaids holding sparklers just before the cake appeared.

including Aerin Lauder and Alexandra Miller von Furstenberg—makes a special effort not to put a microphone in guests' faces and embarrass them. But some people, says Arzt, spontaneously turn to the camera and say something from the heart. And that's what he and his talented colleagues like to include.

Tony Arzt is one of an increasing number of sought-after videographers who also work as documentary filmmakers and thus bring an artist's sensibility and a concomitant appreciation for subtlety to the job. Their videos are in fact rather like mini-documentaries, incorporating such professional filmmaking techniques as freeze frames, slow motion and dissolves, while capturing

that neither bride and groom nor guests need sense their presence. Interviews—by far one of the most bothersome tricks of the trade—are increasingly a thing of the past. Tony Arzt, who has filmed the weddings of princesses and movie stars—as well as those of dozens of society brides,

"Some people simply want to document the event; others want the documentation of the event to be a piece of art."

—NINA AUSTEN, *Dallas wedding planner*

The White Album

WEDDING ALBUMS aren't necessarily bound in white leather anymore, although that style is still the most traditional. The covers can be anything from leather to exquisitely handmade fabric to no cover at all: Many brides simply use beautiful boxes to hold loose photographs of their wedding day. Nor are the pictures all uniformly full-page in size. In fact, the most modern approach to album design is similar to that of stylish magazines, replete with double-page shots, panoramic views and a mix of color and black and white.

What makes a great wedding album? Overall, it must hold one's interest from start to finish and tell a story that can be conveyed without a single written word. It offers variety in design and picture sizes, from quarter- to full-page.

And take heed: Every photo taken does not have to be included. Right after the wedding, you will undoubtedly feel so close to the event that you want to include a shot of every single moment. A month later, you may be willing to let go, at least a little. So do yourself

and everyone else a favor and finalize the editing over a period of several weeks.

That said, be sure to include all the people who are most important to the celebration. Table shots of every single table are necessary only if a bride feels that every single person should be included in the album. An alternate idea is to have your photographer take a shot of every guest as he or she enters the reception. Send each a copy along with your thank-you notes, and keep a set for yourself.

the sounds—the toasts, the music, the tinkle of a glass broken underfoot—that would otherwise be lost forever. Establishing a sense of place is also important in transforming videotape into a polished work. When Arzt shot a wedding on Nantucket, he took a sunrise helicopter ride to get aerial views of the island, which had been a part of the bride's family life for decades. He also keeps striking footage of New York City at all hours of the day and night to add ambiance to his New York wedding videos.

Like a still photographer, a good videographer will also plan ahead, placing a preproduction phone call to the bride to discuss what she wants so he or she knows where to position the cameras. Some set up remote-controlled cameras—spray-painted or otherwise camouflaged—to help keep the process unobtrusive. An ideal wedding video preserves the highlights of the wedding, capturing the spirit and flavor of the occasion, but not every single moment of the action. Like photographers, videographers often work in pairs so they can film as many spontaneous moments as possible and get different angle shots at the same time. But editing is of key importance. Any video that you intend

New York photographer Sarah Merians hand tints her black-and-white images to create a more artistic result. She also likes to use the city as a background, assuming "the bride is willing to risk getting her dress a little messed up."

The wedding is over, you've just unpacked from the honeymoon, but the excitement continues—because the video has arrived! You and your new husband cozy up for a private viewing and then invite your families over the next night for another show. The following week you play it for your best friends. And then, it becomes a habit: Every time someone walks into your house, you offer to "run the videotape."

Try to remember that although your video is likely to seem Oscar-worthy to you, your friends may not be as vitally interested in it, but will also be too polite to decline a viewing. Two suggestions: Have your videographer make you a half-hour version that captures the highlights of the five-hour affair, or offer an "edited" showing of the full-length video ("you probably don't want to see the whole thing") and make sure to keep one finger on the fast-forward button. Limit the viewing to fifteen to thirty minutes, depending upon your guests' level of interest.

to show friends and family shouldn't run more than two hours (although you can certainly ask for an uncut version for your own viewing).

Of course, a videographer is not required. And neither is a professional photographer—at least if you have the courage of Andrea Marcovicci. This singer and actress wanted neither when she married Daniel Reichert. "We're both performers and always feel as though we're on stage," she says. "We didn't want to feel that way on our wedding day." Instead, the couple encouraged friends to bring their own cameras. "It was wonderful, because for months after, we'd receive pictures in the mail. They were the best wedding gifts of all."

Wedding Style: Candid Camera

VALERIE ROZEN PUT so much thought into every aspect of her wedding that her female guests (married or simply longing to be) all admit to envying the results. The affair, held at Industria, a Manhattan loft normally used for professional photo shoots, was a summer event that people talked about throughout the following winter. "I wish I'd thought of that!" was the most oft-repeated comment, whether about the flowers (overgrown, romantic and festooned everywhere), about the personal touches (Valerie and Michael emceed their own wedding) or later, about the couple's wedding album.

The memories of that summer evening were captured by photographer Terry Gruber, whose journalistic approach to documenting the occasion meant not asking anyone to pose and not worrying about perfect lighting (as a photo studio, Industria already has excellent lighting). Rozen had two other important requests of Gruber: "Use only black-and-white film and—I mean this in the nicest possible way—I don't want to know you are at my wedding." Her interest, explains the bride, who has helped raise funds for the International Center for Photography, "is photography as photojournalism as art." And that's why she chose the black-and-white format: "It's artful, romantic and immensely flattering—and it adds a sense of history to the pictures."

The Rozens also chose an untraditional album, covered with a beautiful Italian paper. Gruber organized it into separate "chapters" devoted

Valerie and Michael Rozen felt strongly that they didn't want any posed shots during the course of their wedding (left and below).

to the preparations, the ceremony, the bridal party, the two families joining together and the reception. Each chapter begins with one of the great candid shots the photographer took of the newly married couple. "Terry caught so many spontaneous moments," the bride recalls. "One of my favorites is of us sitting at our table, taken from afar. You can see all the details of my dress, and Michael is throwing back his head, laughing."

The album is quite popular among friends who visit the Rozens' New York townhouse. "People react to it with longing," says the bride. "They all wish they had done what we did. But either their mothers wouldn't let them or they were too scared to stray from a more conventional look." Valerie has stuck with the nontraditional look, however. In fact, Gruber was invited back to photograph the couple's son and daughter shortly after their births—in black and white, of course.

Allowing Terry Gruber to photograph her as she got dressed gave Valerie a photographic chronicle of her last few moments of single life.

Chapter 10
JUST DESSERTS

Here Comes the Cake

Perri Peltz and husband, Eric Ruttenberg.

"FROM THE MOMENT my husband, Eric, proposed, there was no question that Sylvia Weinstock was going to bake my wedding cake. I'd seen her cakes all my adult life and was in love with them. When it came time to choose, I took my mother to meet her, and then my grandmother. I kept going back, because the decision was so delicious. We spent hours discussing the colors of the flowers and the flavors for the filling. Planning that cake was like planning a little wedding."

PERRI PELTZ, *national news correspondent*

WELL BEFORE THE ELEVATOR reaches the cozy third floor of Sylvia Weinstock's New York townhouse, the aroma of baking cake is so intense that it makes visitors want to pick up a fork before the doors even open. This irresistible scent, sadly, won't last until the wedding day—but it is a special treat for the bride who comes to choose her cake. On any given weekday in Weinstock's kitchen/studio, a visitor might encounter five fabulous wedding cakes in various stages of baking and decoration, all in preparation for the coming weekend. And anyone familiar with the pint-size baker—who is tinier than some of her multi-tier creations—knows not to expect the ordinary. One of the latest Weinstock feats? A wedding cake in the form of a vintage Rolls Royce. The icing is pure silver leaf; the inside is chocolate. The bride, crafted of edible sugar dough, wearing a pink wedding gown and a loony expression, is hanging out of the passenger's window; the groom, wearing a gray morning coat and a similar look, is on the driver's side. It's the groom's fourth marriage, Weinstock says with a laugh: "He wanted a little something different this time."

Sylvia Weinstock knows just how to give her customers something different. Her buttercream wedding cakes, in chocolate or any other flavor a couple might dream up, have been on the minds of the marriage-minded since the early 1970s, when she baked her first painstakingly decorated extravaganza. Weinstock is no longer the only cake doyenne reinventing tradition, but she was the first, she set the standard and she is arguably the most famous. To the great good fortune of brides everywhere, Weinstock has also inspired a generation of disciples to creative heights, raising the cake to the level of sculpture: edible art that is not just dessert, but the crowning glory of an already stupendous wedding.

Thanks to Weinstock's impact, good taste (in style and flavor) is now fashionable for wedding cakes. Gone is the era of the plain white cake with white frosting, topped with figures of bride and groom. You can order a cake that is completely customized, from sugar blossoms handmade to match the bridal flowers to sophisticated fillings (try hazelnut or fresh raspberries). No good cake maker would even think of beginning the process without a lengthy meeting to listen to all the details of your

A signature Sylvia Weinstock cake: stacked tiers with sugar dough flowers.

Wedding planner Pat Kerr hung lights and lit candles to dramatize this grand cake created by the pastry chef at the Grand Wailea Resort in Maui.

wedding because they have so much bearing on the cake. And the taste is as important as the look. Cakes can be baked to stay moist right up until the moment they are served. And how do they look? Well, they're as different as the brides are, and very much the epitome of each individual personality.

Designing Women

MANY HOTELS, RESTAURANTS and catering establishments have on-site pastry chefs who create cakes for their in-house weddings. But in recent years a crop of independent bakers have been turning out customized cakes that give the guests something to talk about, as well as to eat. Indeed, it is impossible to do justice to the subject of wedding cakes without considering the creative forces who produce them. Although they can create cakes in almost any shape, size and style, most of these cake makers tend to have a signature look, which is part of the appeal. Their cakes may suit the bride perfectly; but they have a bit of the baker's personality in them, too. A look at some of the artists behind the cakes also provides a look at some of the wide-ranging styles that are possible today—as their designs are ultimately adapted by bakers everywhere.

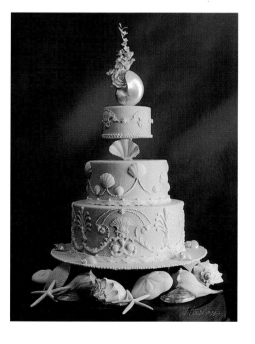

Sylvia Weinstock, Sylvia Weinstock Cakes, *New York City***:** The mother of them all. Brides ranging from Kennedys and Trumps to Middle Eastern royalty, models, movie stars and moguls flock to Weinstock because she is up to any challenge: an uncommon flower blossom, a particular texture, a humorous scene, a subtle or unexpected flavor. Weinstock works with buttercream frosting because she likes the soft finish it creates. Her trademark cake is either stacked or tiered, rising upward of six feet and distinguished by an ethereal look. Incredibly delicate flowers handmade from sugar dough likely cover the exterior. With her signature goggle-like eyeglasses, which cover much of her face, and the towering cakes, Weinstock makes an indelible impression. As do her opinions: The baker offers advice on everything from handling your mother ("It's your wedding, even if she thinks it's hers") to what to serve with the wedding cake ("Nothing. People who spend money on extra desserts should just show all their guests their bankbooks. It's a waste of money— wedding cake is the dessert").

Betty Baird, Sweet Tiers, *Palm Beach***:** Betty Baird breaks a lot of wedding-cake rules. Most bakers decorate their

Many Florida brides opt for Sweet Tier's cakes because baker Betty Baird uses shell motifs, making the beach seem all the more elegant and appropriate for a wedding.

cakes according to the season, she says. But in Florida, you can have a summertime feel all year long. Seashells are one of this baker's most popular motifs. Baird makes molds from real shells, filling them with chocolate, gum paste or sugar dough. She has also given cakes a tropical look with edible palm trees, complete with miniature coconuts. "Color is what turns a cake like that into a birthday cake," Baird notes. "So we do everything in ivories, creams and whites."

Cecile Gady, Cakework, *San Francisco*: Gady has a favorite medium: white chocolate, which she sculpts into edible flowers, ribbons and bows. One of her newest techniques relies on computer technology to recreate logos, photographs, monograms and other designs that she transfers onto sheets of the chocolate. One fabulous Gady cake was marbleized with the swirling patterns of Florentine paper—edible, of course.

Linda Goldsheft, The Cake Studio, *Los Angeles*: This Rhodesian-born cake-maker formerly worked in graphic design, an art that is evident in her fondant-covered cakes. Goldsheft molds her cakes into a variety of shapes: oval, hexagonal, square and the traditional round. She is apt to top them with "creatures"—butterflies, hummingbirds or bees—all made from gum paste. One masterpiece: a six-foot-high cake in the form of the Eiffel Tower, which was designed for actor Blair Underwood's wedding. (Underwood proposed to his wife at the Parisian landmark.) Gum-paste figures of the bride and groom were placed inside the tower.

Goldsheft is also known for wrapping cakes in white chocolate and can "corset" and "drape" a cake so that it resembles the bride's wedding dress down to the frosted lace. Goldsheft's mother served baked Alaska at her wedding instead of wedding cake. "In Rhodesia [now Zimbabwe and Zambia]," she notes, "wedding cakes aren't quite as big as they are here."

Joyce Maynor, Fantasy Frostings, *Whittier, California*: This experienced baker, whose children and grandchildren work right alongside her, has gained fame

Cecile Gady's specialty is printing graphics—yes, graphics—onto white chocolate cakes. These are all entirely edible.

This Joyce Maynor cake features atypical square tiers lavished with her favorite cake covering—fondant.

in recent years from the cakes she bakes for Hollywood weddings. Flowers and leaves are a Maynor specialty: She festoons entire cakes with edible roses, lilies or ivy so that every inch of icing is covered. Even when she makes a traditional white version, the look is magnificent. Maynor once baked for actors John and Rebecca Stamos a cake that was completely white—angel food filled with white chocolate—and featured hundreds of handmade white roses cascading down the sides. It took a hundred hours to complete.

Angie Bennett Mosier, *Atlanta*: Mosier's cakes are rarely towering. Rather, her specialties are sweetness, simplicity and freshness, especially when it comes to the flowers. Women often get married in the spring in Atlanta, where this baker creates her exclusive designs. And in the spring, the gardens of Georgia are exquisite, so Mosier prefers to decorate her butter cakes with buttercream and fresh flowers. She has even been known to cut an armful from a bride's own family garden on the morning of the wedding, then return to her kitchen to arrange them on the finished cake. Talk about fresh!

Romantic and innovative, this Angie Mosier original features a cake inside an edible white chocolate box.

Other Concepts

THE BOLD AND the Beautiful: "I have brides who prefer dots and stripes and a cake that looks straight out of *Alice in Wonderland*," says Betty Baird. Or all chocolate, inside and out. Baird believes that only especially brave brides ice a wedding cake in chocolate because many people think a white wedding cake is as sacred as a white wedding dress.

Individual Cakes: It's an utter fantasy—serving each and every guest his or her own miniature version of a wedding cake. It's also an increasingly popular choice, although this delectable trend involves intense labor and certainly hikes up the cost considerably. Each cake must be decorated individually, as if it were the only wedding cake; Betty Baird has made as many as three hundred for one occasion. The delivery alone might take four trucks. That said, brides and guests alike love them. Cecile Gady has baked "wild and wacky" individual wedding cakes, in a zebra or a leopard print, and once made three-inch miniature wedding cakes—each housed under glass and wrapped in a gold box—as wedding favors.

New York fashion observer Lillian Wang, who was wed in Napa Valley, didn't want any cake at all until friends persuaded her to serve individual cakes. "I didn't like the whole ceremony of cutting the cake and feeding it to each other," she says. Instead, the bride served chocolate cupcakes with chocolate frosting made by Sam Godfrey of Perfect Endings,

Sam Godfrey of Perfect Endings created this charming tower of cupcakes (opposite) for bride Lillian Wang, who wanted something untraditional and whimsical.

"Anything a bride wants, we can do these days. We try to keep things one of a kind. Artistically, we can get way out there."

—CECILE GADY, *San Francisco cake baker*

BUTTERCREAM: a smooth mixture of powdered sugar whipped with butter, and often with egg whites and vanilla (every baker has his or her own secret recipe). Tastes like whipped cream. Used for icing, filling and decoration.

FONDANT: a thick, creamy, sugar-based icing that is dense and chewy, with a perfectly smooth consistency. Poured fondant gives the cake a shiny alabaster finish and rounded edges. Rolled fondant has a matte finish.

GANACHE: a heavenly combination of chocolate and heavy cream. When warm, it is thin enough to be poured over a cake and will remain dark and shiny. It can also be cooled and beaten to a lighter color and thicker consistency.

GUM PASTE: used to create flowers and other cake decorations. Has a consistency similar to fondant's, but is definitely not meant for consumption.

MARZIPAN: a sweetened almond paste that can be rolled, cut and molded into decorations or rolled and draped as icing.

ROYAL ICING: made from meringue and powdered sugar and whipped very stiff. Used in old-fashioned pastry bags to decorate cakes with flowers, delicate piping and the like. Edible.

SUGAR DOUGH: similar in consistency to gum paste, but edible. Rolled, cut and molded into decorations.

STACKED CAKE: features layers stacked directly, one on top of another.

TIERED CAKE: has layers separated by columns.

WRAPPED CHOCOLATE: chocolate (usually white) that is melted, then wrapped around the cake for a seamless finish.

---

each with a different-colored flower on top. A stylist arranged them on a multi-level circular table, adding flowerpots with fresh flowers and ribbons. The arrangement was gorgeous, recalls Wang, who was delighted to see guests walk up to the table, pick up a cupcake and eat it standing or sitting. "The biggest fans of all were the children," she says. "They loved it."

Completely Custom: Offbeat requests are almost always taken, provided the baker and the bride have the same comic sensibility. Cecile Gady once made a tie-dyed cake for a couple devoted to the rock band Grateful Dead. Betty Baird has baked cakes that are lopsided. ("All the tiers are crooked: It's a hoot.") Though a good cake baker typically transforms sugar dough or gum paste or royal icing into gardens of earthly delight, he or she should also be up to the creative challenges modern brides present.

To each her own. Creative cakes (opposite, clockwise from top left): Sylvia Weinstock's gazebo; Polly's Cakes' cutting edge 6-tier cake-in-the-round; Sam Godfrey's five-tier cake with fresh fruit and flower adornments; and a cake made to look like a stack of wedding presents from Colette's Cakes.

Piece of Cake

DESPITE THE OLD AXIOM, you *can* have your cake and eat it, too. Today's wedding cakes aren't just good—they're delicious. Though many brides still serve additional desserts, the cakes truly are flavorful enough to be dessert all by themselves. Acknowledging the sophisticated palates of their sophisticated brides, cake bakers are turning their creative minds to the insides of cakes as well as the decoration. They keep cakes moister by baking one layer at a time so that they don't dry out in the oven. Last-minute baking also helps; some cake makers start on Thursdays before a Saturday affair; others work into the wee hours of the morning of the wedding day. The heavy frostings, such as buttercream and fondant, that are now fashionable help to seal in moistness and taste.

There is also an endless array of choices for both fillings and cake flavors. One of Joyce Maynor's specialties is chocolate fudge surprise: fudge cake with cream ganache, crushed toffee and dark chocolate mousse. Jane Lockhart, of Sweet Lady Jane bakers near Los Angeles, offers a triple berry cake with fresh berries only; canned fruit and jams are out of the question. Two of Cecile Gady's best sellers are a banana truffle cake and an almond cake with vanilla cream and raspberries. Sylvia Weinstock offers carrot cake; among her fillings are hazelnut and chocolate mousse. And Betty Baird makes the decision process much easier for the bride. She specializes in a half-and-half cake. One layer is butter pound cake, one layer is chocolate and every guest is served a piece of both.

Choosing a wedding cake is actually not a piece of cake. So many options exist these days that it's easy to get a little overwhelmed. Just as you do with your wedding gown, you will probably spend a lot of time dreaming about your cake. It's a significant part of the wedding fantasy. Expect to have that two-hour consultation with your baker, ask for tastes of the myriad cakes and fillings and look through the portfolios for ideas. A baker will likely request color swatches (tablecloths, napkins, even drapery), flower samples and a picture of your wedding dress. Most professionals begin with a stock list of questions about the type of wedding the bride is planning. Season is one consideration: A baker's rule of thumb is that chocolate always tastes better in winter; a lighter, fruit-filled cake is delicious in the summer. You should also discuss the dessert course. If there is going to be another chocolate dessert, for instance, you shouldn't serve chocolate wedding cake. The same goes for fruit. Don't worry about coordinating the cake with the rest of the menu, however. Wedding cake is special enough to go with any meal. And as with most other decisions during the wedding, you should aim for the best-quality cake, not the showiest. "Don't wear all your jewelry at one time," explains Sylvia Weinstock. "The cake doesn't have to have everything but the kitchen sink on it."

A Cake of His Own

MOST GROOMS GET the picture about two minutes after they propose: The wedding is for the bride. That said, an old southern tradition that gives the groom something of his own on the wedding day is coming back into style: a cake. This so-called groom's cake is typically much smaller than the couple's wedding cake and designed in a whimsical way to represent his occupation or favorite pastime. Most often, it's in the shape of an airplane, a golf course, a fish or a boat. And it's almost always chocolate. The groom's cake is customarily served at the same time as the wedding cake or the night before the wedding, at the rehearsal dinner. Occasionally, it is

Designed by Cake Studio in Los Angeles, a cake for a dog-loving groom.

displayed at the wedding, cut, then put in individual boxes for each guest to take home. The idea is that all the unmarried women are to place the cake under their pillows that night to dream of their true love. (Sounds a little messy—and besides, today's version tastes so good that not to eat it is a shame.)

Most important, the groom's cake usually brings a sense of humor to the wedding or rehearsal dinner. For one groom who was a body-builder, Cecile Gady baked a chocolate-glazed cake with gold- and silver-leaf barbells all over it. For a duck hunter, she made a cake of ducks lined up in a row. Wedding planner Mindy Weiss truly likes to give the guys something to laugh about. Her most recent inspiration? A cake in the shape of a tractor for one groom crazy about farm equipment—a figure of the bride was in the driver's seat, and the groom was in the scooper.

cakes themselves—quite detailed and luxe—demand something a little less obvious. Crowning a cake with something that is already decorating it, such as fresh flowers or bows, is often the most appealing option.

There are exceptions, however. Pastry wizard Rebecca Russell actually makes bridal couples out of marzipan. Brides can choose from the generic variety (designed to look like "everybride and everygroom") or the portrait type. Supply Russell with a picture of the bride and groom, as well as a photo of the bride's wedding dress, and she can make a lifelike replica (matching dress and all) to top the cake. After the wedding, the figures can be saved for years as long as they're encased in glass. Bride-and-groom cake toppers are fashionable again because they reflect the personalization of today's weddings, Russell explains. Of course, they don't have to appear on top of the cake—you can place them on the cake table or even on the escort card table.

What Goes on Top?

THE ANSWER USED TO BE universal: porcelain or plastic figures of the bride and groom. Today, most bakers don't think the figures are attractive enough to top their cakes. Not to mention that the

One Year Later

THE TRADITION OF saving the top of the cake for a couple's first anniversary is a subject of debate among bakers. "My brides tell me it's still delicious one year later," says Sylvia Weinstock. She suggests putting it in the freezer for an hour right after the wedding to harden the icing, then wrapping it tightly in first, plastic wrap, and finally, either a plastic bag or a plastic container before refreezing. But Linda Goldsheft, who disagrees, doesn't encourage anyone to keep anything in a freezer for a year. "In fact, many couples tell me that they were so hungry when they got back to their room," the baker says, "they just ate the cake right then and there!" Betty Baird has the ultimate solution. One year later, she bakes her brides a smaller anniversary cake that mimics the top tier of their wedding cake. "Every weekend, I make at least three or four anniversary cakes," Baird says. "It's a nice way of keeping in touch."

> *"To me, every bride is a princess. And I'm wholly aware that, to her parents, she's a queen. That's why everybody gets a cake worthy of royalty."*
>
> —SYLVIA WEINSTOCK, *New York cake baker*

Nosegays of fresh flowers are also lovely toppers: Angie Bennett Mosier once put them in the bride's silver christening cup. Steuben Glass makes a pair of crystal swans that can be engraved with the couple's initials. Finally, vintage figures saved from a mother's or grandmother's cake are always a nice touch. Or go to flea markets—and look for a bride and groom that resemble you.

Presentation and Ceremony

MOST WEDDING CAKES require assembly—and often the baker arrives to put it all together on the day of the wedding. Usually, it's a matter of connecting the tiers and adding the toppers. But with some cakes, the assembly can be quite complicated. Joyce Maynor once flew a very intricate hexagonal cake, the layers packed in ice, to the Middle East after spending two months working on its design and creation. Made for a Saudi Arabian princess, this Maynor masterpiece was decorated with fragile latticework and snowflakes. The base alone measured forty-eight inches across. Not only did the baker have to check the cake at the airport; she also had to leave it in an airport freezer during an overnight layover in New York. ("I didn't sleep at all that night," she admits.) Once in Saudi Arabia, the layers

were assembled in a few days: With a few touchups, the cake looked as if it had been delivered from her California bakery a few blocks away.

When a cake is designed to make a statement, it should receive the proper attention no matter how far it travels. A wedding cake is traditionally displayed throughout the reception, and people should look at it longer than the few seconds when the bride and groom cut a slice. As Sylvia Weinstock says: "It should literally be put on a pedestal." To heighten the effect, bakers or florists (or both together) usually dress up the table with fresh flowers or petals for its presentation. One of Cecile Gady's creations went further than that. Designed for a couple crazy about butterflies, one of her cakes featured fluttering images of the creatures printed onto white chocolate—and was displayed in a birdbath.

The wedding cake should also be served in a grand manner. After all, it is no ordinary dessert. The cake, usually the last thing guests eat at the reception, symbolizes the sweetness of life and wishes the newlyweds good luck. If possible, the presentation should include some festivity, too. Gady once baked individual cakes for every table at a wedding. When it was time to serve them, she put Fourth of July sparklers in each one and had the waiters march from the kitchen as if they were in a parade.

Etiquette

At some point after the wedding cake makes its grand entrance, tradition dictates that the bride cut a piece and feed a bite to the groom; then he feeds a bite to her. The act represents their first shared sweet moment as a married couple, and it should be handled with a certain amount of decorum. In fact, today's brides eschew the age-old groom's tradition of smashing a piece of cake into the bride's face, deeming it immature. Los Angeles wedding planner Mindy Weiss swears she can always tell how long a marriage is going to last by the way a groom feeds the cake to his bride. "If he's gentle and doesn't let the cake get on the bride's dress, they're going to be okay," she says. "If he smashes it in her face: divorce." The moment should always be in good taste, but it can have some humor. "One groom put icing on the bride's nose and licked it off," recalls Weiss, "and I got the feeling that they were going to have a very happy, funny life together."

Feeding each other gently, and joyously (opposite), is far more elegant than smearing wedding cake into each other's faces.

Wedding Style: A Cake Fit for a Chef

THOSE WHO KNOW of Sara Whiteford (and thousands in the San Francisco area do) expected the gourmet chef and best-selling cookbook author to bake her own wedding cake when the time came. Sara and her twin sister, Mary, are the co-owners of the catering company Thymes Two, and their stylish cuisine—featured in newspapers, on television and on the epicurean Web site cooking.com—has earned them considerable celebrity on the West Coast. The duo had already collaborated on Mary's cake, an

Though she had only one bite of
her stupendous six-tier cake (above),
bride Sara Whiteford knew it was
"perfection—inside and out."

Sara and Erick Whiteford posed in front of the grand fireplace, a focal point in their ballroom. Soon after the ceremony, the cake was positioned there so all the guests could admire its beauty.

eleven-tiered production decorated with no fewer than seventeen hundred gum-paste flowers personally hand-molded by the twins. "We even made a gazebo to display it in," recalls Sara. "It took forever." So when it came to her own wedding cake, she says, she was ready to abdicate.

But who was enough of a perfectionist to create a wedding cake for, well, a perfectionist? "Entertaining is ingrained in my soul," explains Sara, who wed sports marketer Erick Whiteford in the Merchants Exchange Building, a downtown San Francisco landmark. "I felt a lot of pressure," admits the bride, fully aware that her guests had high expectations for the wedding menu. Inspiration hit when Sara saw a cake created by her colleague, pastry chef Sam Godfrey of Perfect Endings, for a wedding at the Coppola Vineyards in Napa Valley. "When I found out it was Sam's design," she says of the multi-tiered production, which incorporated several stunning layers of fresh roses, "I had to call him. I love that larger-than-life effect: I wanted my cake to be grandiose."

Sara got her wish. The Whitefords' wedding cake featured six tiers of cake—separated by another six tiers of very tight, very perfect rosebuds in different shades of red (and a few yellows) to echo the wedding's overall color theme. It towered. It stunned the crowd. It stole the show. And it was perfectly suited to the elegant interior of the Merchants Exchange, which is distinguished by high ceilings and enormous fireplaces. "We exchanged vows right in front of the biggest fireplace, and as soon as we left that spot, the cake was wheeled into it," recalls Sara. Displayed on a gold-rimmed mirror atop a gold damask tablecloth, it became an instant focal point. "You could see it from almost any angle in the room. It was a masterpiece."

Moreover, Godfrey made sure the inside tasted as good as the outside looked. His innovative recipe specified different flavors in the different layers—including tiers of carrot cake, a layer or two of rich chocolate and caramel, and another filled with silky white chocolate and California apricots. "The waiters just passed around small pieces and our guests tasted them all," says Sara, who regrets that she managed to eat just the one bite that her new husband fed to her during the cake-cutting ceremony. As for saving the top layer to eat on their first anniversary, as tradition dictates? "We didn't bother," the bride says. "Being a chef, I'm not one to eat frozen food—even a piece of the most beautiful wedding cake in the world."

In order to enjoy being the bride, Sara, getting ready to walk down the aisle, had to relinquish the titles of "chef" and "baker" for the night.

Chapter 11

BEAUTY AND THE BRIDE

Evelyn and Leonard Lauder.

Getting the Glow

"I GOT MARRIED at the Plaza in 1959, but it feels like yesterday. My mother-in-law, Estée, said she wanted to do my makeup. She didn't want me to wear too much. We used a little bit of eye shadow, a pale one, which was very chic in those days, and some mascara and just a little blush. And I wore a very pretty, subtle lipstick. I didn't wear any makeup base or powder. I was so young and my skin was so smooth. I looked very natural. After the ceremony, Leonard, my husband, said he had never seen anyone as beautiful. He said he knew for sure."

EVELYN LAUDER, *cosmetics executive*

ALL BRIDES ARE BEAUTIFUL. But how they get that way is the real story.

The white dress, the glow of pearls, the aura of love, the sheer adrenaline rushing through her veins as she walks down the aisle: All this helps to make each bride gorgeous. All this—and more. The pre-wedding facial and massage, the manicure (the better to show off the ring), the pedicure (for the honeymoon), the makeup artist, the perfect hue of lipstick. There is no question that the amount of effort most brides put into the way they look on their wedding day can reach extremes. But think about it: For most brides, this is the one and only time in their lives that one hundred or more pairs of eyes are watching every move they make. Not to mention that you want your future husband to be astounded by your ravishing beauty as you walk toward him (and a lifetime, one hopes, of mutual admiration). You don't want your guests to say, "She was the only bride I've ever seen who didn't have, you know, that glow." And you do want your grandchildren to look at your photographs and acknowledge that yes, at one time, you were gorgeous.

Ah, the pressure. Most brides are very, very nervous, confirms Liz Michael, a New York cosmetics consultant who's made up dozens of jittery brides. Yet what she finds bizarre is that most brides are not nervous about getting married, but about looking great. Perhaps that is because mere moments before you walk down the aisle everything

A bride should consult a professional makeup artist in the months before her wedding and definitely schedule a practice session to choose colors.

besides making sure your lipstick is on your lips (not on your teeth) is likely too BIG to ponder. Furthermore, you should have answered all those other questions (Is he really the one for me?) well beforehand.

Golden Rules of Bridal Beauty

THE MOST IMPORTANT aspect of bridal beauty—keeping it simple—is the most difficult for brides to embrace. Because the wedding dress is so different from what a woman wears every other day of her life, most brides believe that their makeup should be dramatically different, too. That shouldn't be the case. The dress should say "wedding." Your face, however, should say "you," but in a slightly enhanced version of your everyday self. Don't give in to the temptation to pile on the makeup. You don't want to look like someone you're not—especially to your

fiancé when he is just moments away from tying the knot. But don't go au naturelle either (remember: the photos, the photos). In fact, spring for a professional makeup artist, and definitely plan at least one practice session before the wedding.

More important, don't try something new. To be perfectly clear: Do not cut your hair dramatically, perm it or color it a shade not typically found in nature. One otherwise levelheaded New York attorney we know dyed her naturally gorgeous auburn hair a Lucille Ball red two weeks before her wedding for some reason she still cannot adequately explain. It took the full two weeks—and several hysterical visits to her hairdresser—to return her color to normal. "It did take my mind off the larger issues," she says now. Yes, but so would a day at a local spa.

Along the same lines: Don't try a new face cream, because you could break out; don't try to get a suntan, because you could get burned; and don't try a new brand of cosmetic anytime close to the wedding because you could have an allergic reaction. Finally, don't be unrealistic. You don't want to look like Cindy Crawford on her wedding day (well, maybe you do), because you're not Cindy Crawford. You want to look like yourself, only better than you've ever looked in your life.

Saying "I Do... Need Makeup"

BRIDES WHO CAN AFFORD to hire a professional makeup artist are strongly urged to do so; and the bride should definitely plan on having at least one practice session before the wedding day. Professionals can advise about the types of makeup that will look best indoors or out, in day or evening, and in natural or artificial light. They are also knowledgeable about cosmetics that will stand up should the bride sweat, cry or be kissed by hundreds of people. (All three are highly probable.) Most important, they know how to apply makeup for a flattering effect in photographs—which doesn't necessarily mean more makeup, but rather the right kind and application. That said, you shouldn't be intimidated about suggesting the kind of makeup you prefer. Feel free to bring your own cosmetics to the first run-through. You may want to combine them with the artist's inventory. Even more important than the makeup is the absolute priority that the bride feel comfortable. Here are some other necessities in the makeup department:

The Foundation of a Good Marriage (Face): Foundation is a must, even if you don't wear it every day. Blotches show up in photographs, and who wants to remember them for a lifetime? If you are used to wearing foundation, don't change it for the wedding. If you aren't, head for a beauty counter and have an expert match the right foundation to your skin type and color.

Getting the Glow: "Don't jump up and down," advises Liz Michael. (Some brides have been known to do this.) "It will just make you red. Don't pinch your cheeks either—they'll just get blotchy." What can you do? For the perfect "I'm-in-love" glow, look for the tinted, but sheer, foundations produced by such top-of-the-line cosmetics companies as Clinique, Prescriptives and Lancôme; these are

A bride's wedding day is perhaps the one and only time in her life that so many people will be focusing on her—and her alone.

appropriate for both day and evening weddings. Pearlescent eye shadows and blushes add subtle shimmer and can also be used on your lips, under lip gloss and even in your cleavage.

You Can Cry If You Want To: Why? Because waterproof mascara has never been more effective. Quick tips: Apply more mascara to the middle of lashes, less on the ends, and never use it on the lower lid. And dab quickly at tears; don't smear. Or try pulling your lower lid down and holding it for a few seconds so that it forms a pocket to catch the tears. (Don't even think about doing this during the ceremony.) And two cautionary words about eyeglasses: glare proof.

Before Kissing the Groom: Weddings must be the reason the cosmetics industry has created so many long-lasting lipsticks: They're perfect for one's wedding day. (What bride remembers to reapply?) The newest formulas last longer, and many contain vitamins, such as the moisturizing E. If you're stuck on a shade that is not made in a long-lasting formula, professional makeup artist Trish McEvoy suggests outlining your lips with a lip pencil of the same or a similar color and then filling in with the pencil. Apply lipstick. Blot. Apply again. One of the worst mistakes brides make is wearing lipstick in too pale a shade. A veil or other headpiece can make you appear a bit top-heavy, and more lip color helps offset this effect.

New endurance lipstick formulations enable a bride to kiss all day—like Molly Duffy with Hugh Burns (right)—and rarely reapply.

Absolute Must-Have: An oil-controlling powder. When you're anxious, even dry skin will produce sebum, and shine shows up in photographs. Oil-blotting papers are great for last-minute fixes and free you from adding more makeup.

The Bridal Beauty Schedule

WHEN SHOULD YOU have that pre-wedding facial? How do you get that bridal glow if you have

Now is also the time to start a regular facial regimen (once a month). Find a good skin-care product that agrees with you and stay with it. A smart option might be a multi-acid moisturizer. The gentle alpha-hydroxy acids they contain are designed to peel away layers of skin marred by fine lines and blemishes gradually, revealing fresh, glowing skin underneath. Also begin, or step up, your exercise program to reduce stress. Start taking care of your hands, because everyone's going to be looking at your ring. Deep conditioning lotions and alpha-hydroxy hand creams can also get you those smooth, "Look! I'm engaged!" hands. And, of course, regular manicures will help. Finally: Breathe, relax, take up yoga.

been more than a little edgy lately, and a lack of sleep has you looking ghostly pale? With all the other wedding details to arrange, it's challenging for a bride to find time to take care of herself. That's why a detailed game plan for your hair and makeup regimens helps. Here's sample schedule of what to do when:

You've gotten engaged: Kiss your fiancé, set a date and then run, don't walk, to your hairdresser. The average engagement is ten months long, and that's how much time you may need for your hair to grow to the right length for your wedding. In fact, most hairdressers agree that this is the time to grow your hair. You can always cut it later, advises the New York stylist Stephen Knoll, but "this way you leave your options open."

Five months before: Schedule appointments with the hairdresser and makeup artist for the day of the wedding and specify that you want them to come to your home if they can. Interview the makeup artist and schedule your first practice session as well. Over the next five months, maintain a good relationship with your chosen hairstylist. Aside from your mother, this is the person you will want to keep closest during the crucial, anxious hours before your wedding. You should have chosen your headpiece by now. Bring a sketch or photograph to your hairdresser so that the two of you can be sure it will work with your chosen hair style. See the stylist once a month for a trim and a deep-conditioning treatment to keep your hair shiny and healthy. If you have

More important than any cosmetic is being as relaxed as possible on one's wedding day. Achieving a look of calm, peaceful reflection—as did Rosemary Carlucci De Mann (above)—is far more beautiful than anything a makeup artist can do.

decided to wear your hair up, try it several times over the next few months. Go out to dinner. Go dancing. Get used to the way it feels.

Three months before: Are you still exercising? One of the newest trends in bridal showers is a weekend at a spa with a few well-chosen girlfriends. It's better for you than a champagne brunch. Schedule a girls-only spa trip now.

Two months before: The most important thing to concentrate on is your skin. If you tend to break out under stress or look sallow when you're tired, consider eliminating coffee, which can make you look sallow. And be sure to drink those eight glasses of water a day for the next two months. Visit your hairdresser for the first run-through and bring the veil or any hair accessories you're planning to wear.

One month before: Have another run-through—this time with both your hair stylist and makeup artist. Make sure to discuss what makeup will hold up in sultry weather or under hot lights. Any new brands should be tried now to test for allergic reaction. With your makeup and hair done, have your wedding photographer take a portrait of you. Pictures are better than the mirror in helping you decide if you like the way you look.

Two weeks before: If you color your hair, do it now to give yourself time to correct any problems. Have your last trim now or at the beginning of next week. Make sure it's a minor one. Try to fit in a few deep-conditioning treatments—either at home or, even better, at the salon—over the course of the next two weeks. Have your last facial (a deep-cleansing one).

The week of: Say you're getting married on Saturday night:

Monday: Confirm appointments with your hairstylist and makeup artist for the wedding day. Buy all the travel-size beauty products you'll need for your honeymoon.

Tuesday: Have all your waxing done, including eyebrows, bikini line and legs. If you're feeling pale, have an invigorating mini-facial, but do not let the beautician do a search-and-destroy mission on your pre-wedding skin. Just ask politely for a face massage and a refreshing mask; request those cool cucumbers for your eyes.

Wednesday: An herbal wrap at a local day spa will help combat water retention. (Make sure you've had lunch first; you don't want to pass out from the combination of compressed heat and hunger.) Treat your hair to that last deep-conditioning treatment.

Thursday: A salt body rub will exfoliate your skin and give you a glow. This is a great treatment for a bride wearing a low-cut or off-the-shoulder wedding dress. Cap off the salt rub with a massage.

Friday: Time for your manicure (pale pink polish or a French manicure is most popular for brides) and pedicure (choose a color you will be able to live with for the duration of the honeymoon). Make sure you have scheduled these appointments late in the day, leaving less time to chip the color or break a nail before the wedding. Some brides leave these appointments for the day of, but why chance it? If you ruin a nail after a last-minute manicure there may not be time to fix it. Purchase and pack matching polish for touch-ups.

The day before: Stick to your usual skin regimen. Don't try a last-minute beautifying mask now, because it could give you an unexpected rash. Another massage would be divine. Despite what all the famous models say about alcohol being bad for your skin, one little glass of Chardonnay might just be the ticket to a good night's sleep.

The day of: If you're having an afternoon wedding, you'll probably have to rise at the crack of down. Oh well, adrenaline will keep you going. If yours is an evening wedding, sleep late if at all possible. Then, eat a well-balanced lunch packed with protein and carbohydrates. Face it: You're unlikely to be eating much dinner. Schedule your hair and make-up team to arrive at the same time. Allow about three hours for the beauty regimen and for getting dressed. Don't condition your hair today or it will be too limp to work

Most photographers today like a bride to look a little imperfect—wind rustling hair or a finger wiping away a tear makes a woman seem more real.

with. Hairstyling should be done first, but the make-up artist can start when/if your hair is in rollers. If you need to cry, do it before you start with the makeup. "I always tell my brides to have a good cry early in the day," says veteran wedding planner Marcy Blum. "Then there's time for the puffiness to subside." An additional beauty secret from Ellen Gendler, a Manhattan dermatologist: An ice pack or a washcloth doused in whole milk can reduce redness or puffiness.

If you're having photographs taken before the ceremony, make sure to leave time for freshening up before you walk down the aisle. Most important, try to find a few minutes alone. After all that hard work, you should have the opportunity to see yourself in the mirror as a bride.

Smile...Though Your Heart Is Pounding

NEXT TO MAKEUP ARTISTS, wedding photographers give the best beauty advice. After all, they're the individuals you are trusting to capture the moment for posterity. You should listen to them if they think your lipstick is too dark, your forehead is too shiny, your eyes are filled with panic . . . .

Learn from what some of the most experienced have to say.

Alan Berliner, Los Angeles: My pet peeve is flowers pinned in a bride's hair. Invariably, they fly off during the first dance and the bride winds up looking like a mess. And I absolutely insist that you hire a makeup artist. No matter how talented you are at applying makeup, you won't be able to handle it on your wedding day.

Lucy Brown, Upperville, Virginia: Under-eye concealer will make you look like an owl, and the flash exacerbates that effect. Flash also illuminates a slip under a dark dress, so bridesmaids should make sure that their slips are the same color as their dresses.

Margaret Busk, Chicago: Don't worry about positioning your head. Good photographers will take any number of versions of the same shot and will inevitably capture the most natural composition at some point. Also, brides should beware of too much jewelry, which can compete for attention.

Leslie Corrado, San Francisco: Shine is the worst. I also like to be in charge of the powder and lipstick; I carry it for the bride and give it to her to reapply before the toast. I even powder grooms. My advice about posture: Always put your weight on your back foot, because this makes you stand more naturally. And finally, when you shop for your wedding makeup, wear something white.

Denis Reggie, Atlanta and New York: Think of your makeup as something you would wear on a date at night. Nothing more. The film we use nowadays can capture the subtleties of the most natural-looking makeup. Also, wear your shoes a few times before your wedding. They can alter your posture if you're not comfortable. And try to understand that the need for reality far exceeds the need for perfection. It's acceptable to have a strand of hair out of place.

Julie Skarratt, New York: Hair is always best when it's pulled off the face. If it hangs in your face, it can create a shadow. And don't worry about crying—it makes for lovely pictures. Recently I photographed a wedding where the groom fainted and the bride cried. I shot it all. They can decide later if they want the pictures; I hope those shots will give them a good laugh.

After all the hard work of getting ready, a bride should leave herself a few moments before the ceremony to look in the mirror and savor what she sees.

Wedding Style: A Tale of Two Brides

THIS IS A TALE OF TWO beautiful brides: one entering a first marriage, the other a second. The former pulled out all the stops to ensure she looked radiant; the latter hardly did anything at all. The experience for both, nonetheless, had a common theme. Preparing to look beautiful for their men drew them closer to the women in their lives—mothers, daughters, best friends. And ultimately, the beauty of the day proved more important than the lipstick shades they chose to wear.

Jane Agnew, *Town & Country*'s fashion editor, was married to business entrepreneur Steve Schelling on a crisp October Sunday afternoon in a New Jersey church, with a reception immediately following at a country club. It was a traditional wedding with all the trimmings for this first-time bride.

In the months preceding the wedding, twenty-nine-year-old Agnew threw herself into a beauty quest, or as she called it, "a quest for perfection." She spent countless enjoyable hours in conversation with her mother and married sister about how she should look. She interviewed more than a few hairstylists and makeup artists before settling on one of each. And she scheduled several visits with her trusty maid of honor ("We really bonded over this") to a day spa in Manhattan for facials, wraps and massages, as well as a week-of-the-wedding facial mask to give her that much-desired bridal glow.

Agnew tackled the timing of all her wedding-day beauty appointments with the gusto of a fashion editor overseeing a dozen shoots in one afternoon with a testy model and a testier photographer. Because the wedding would begin at 3 p.m., her hair would be done at 11 a.m., her makeup at 12:30. By 1:15, she'd be ready to slip into her custom-made Badgley Mischka wedding gown. "I work with clothing and models day in and day out," the bride says. "Sometimes I don't even have time to pay attention to the way I look. Now, I'm making up for that."

Jane Agnew Schelling put her all into looking beautiful on her wedding day, with a full retinue of beauty treatments and a staff of professionals at the ready.

For Agnew, one of the most special things about a wedding is seeing a groom look at the bride for the first time. "I want Steve to look at me and say, 'Oh my god, look how gorgeous she looks—and she's going to be my wife!'" said Agnew just a few days before her wedding . Well, he did. And she was. And it was perfect.

Everything that Agnew went through, Ellen Katz did, too. Only, for Katz, it was in the late 1960s, when she was a first-time bride. "I remember sitting under the dryer with rollers on for several hours," she says. "I was very, very nervous."

Not this time around. At forty-nine, Katz, a philanthropist, married Howard Katz, a limited partner at Goldman, Sachs, in a private room at New York City's chic Le Cirque 2000 restaurant, joined by the five children from their previous marriages. Her maid of honor was her twenty-something daughter, Elizabeth; she lunched with college friends days before the wedding in lieu of visits to a day spa; and she applied her wedding-day makeup herself. In fact, Katz followed her typical daily makeup routine, which takes three minutes from start (blusher) to finish (a dab of 24 Fauborg by Hermes), just minutes before the ceremony. "Beauty at my age isn't about one night," she says. "It's a matter of constant maintenance." Katz believes that her daily exercise sessions and the peace she's achieved in her life do a lot more for her looks than any hour spent with a makeup artist could. Her walk down the aisle, escorted by her teenage son, Teddy, was also far different from the first time around: "I felt confident," Katz says, "and that made me feel more beautiful than I've ever felt in my life."

Chapter 12

WEDDING GIFTS

Presents with Presence

"I GOT MARRIED in 1946 in my parents' apartment in Budapest. My husband was part of the American contingent of the Allied control commission. He wore his uniform for the ceremony and looked very handsome. It was right after the war, so we had a very, very small wedding, and I didn't get many gifts. The American boys, my husband's friends, gave us a couple of silver trays, though, that I loved. They were hammered silver, very simple and beautiful. What is amazing to me is that I received them in a different era and in a different country, but I still have them, love them and use them. Now, that's the definition of a good wedding present."

JUDITH LEIBER, *handbag designer*

LIKE JUDITH LEIBER'S silver trays, a truly successful wedding gift is one that endures. It is something a bride will use after one year of marriage and after fifty. Something she will remember as the decades go by. Something she would want to pass on to her children. Something personal, or personalized. Or something that in its daily use or in its very presentation—stainless tableware from a grandparent who bought all the place settings in one grand gesture—will come to have great emotional value over time. Flatware is only flatware, after all, unless it is given with love, as a gift.

Memorable, however, means different things to different people. Consider the young woman who was swept away by a thoughtful wedding present from her mother-in-law: the use of the latter's prized housekeeper, one day a week, for life. (Whose life, is the question.) Then there is the bride and groom who received, respectively, a top-of-the-line sewing kit and an equally high-quality tool kit from the same couple. The bride was initially irritated (how sexist!) and puzzled (after all, they had a tailor and a building super). Yet, years later, the two use their kits more often than they would like to admit, chuckle because they actually own such things and yes, remember that these were the wedding gifts of a very prescient older couple.

The Fine Art of Registering

WHETHER THE CHOICE is personal, whimsical, creative, practical or—like the mother-in-law's housekeeper—all of the above, wedding gifts are tokens of love and goodwill that allow friends and family to share in the celebration. Receiving gifts is part of the anticipation of getting married, and registering for them has long been one of the rituals of the engagement period. Some brides hesitate to register because they don't like the idea of asking for presents, even when the request is indirect. But if you don't list your preferences somewhere, warns wedding planner Marcy Blum, "you're just going to get twenty decanters." In fact, registering is an excellent way for you to express your tastes and interests and is particularly helpful in an era when wedding guests must often choose presents for couples who already have established households.

*An array of superb gardening
tools and books is a perfect
gift for the cultivated couple.*

Fortunately, that choice has never been broader or more imaginative. Traditional china, crystal and flatware are still the most popular items on most registries. (There is certainly nothing like the thrill of the arrival of that first blue box from Tiffany & Company.) But a more creative approach to gift giving means your registries will likely list a selection of up-to-date items as well as the faithful standbys. The current comeback of the cocktail party, for instance, has made martini shakers and all manner of other bar items ranging from shot glasses to brandy snifters fashionable. An interest in Asian culture has done the same for sushi platters and sake sets.

What is more, establishing a registry is no longer limited to the traditional trip to a fine jewelry or department store. In several urban areas, for instance, you will likely find a variation of the innovative Manhattan store known as The Wedding List, where soon-to-be-marrieds can wander through an entire townhouse decorated as if a couple actually

Most brides are happy to receive the essentials. Generally, plates, bowls and pans should be selected from a bride's registry.

lives there. Everything is for sale, and anything can be put on the register. Formal china, including Limoges and Wedgwood, along with crystal and silver, are displayed in the dining room; a library is furnished with books, bar accoutrements and games; the kitchen is fitted with all the best in culinary equipment; and a bedroom showcases linens and luggage. A changing array of antiques and one-of-a-kind objets is designed for the couple who already has everything. This "life come to life" is the perfect example of how stores are modernizing their presentations and their wedding registries for the contemporary bride and groom.

The modern registry is hardly limited to household furnishings, however. Aware that most couples wish their gifts to reflect their interests and lifestyles, some of the most unexpected places now offer wedding registries. If you are an exercise fanatic, check with your health club; many have registries for training sessions and memberships. Some retailers will also allow you to register for treadmills, weights

196

An unusual and memorable gift is one the bride and groom wouldn't buy for themselves, such as these antique glasses and decanters.

and the like. Day spas make it easy for wedding guests to treat stressed-out brides and grooms to massages. If you are a music lover, consider putting your preferences on file at a record or electronics store. Aspiring chefs can register for cooking lessons at culinary schools such as Peter Kump's in Manhattan; neophytes can do the same at community education programs, which offer popular courses with names like "How to Boil Water" for young marrieds. Some couples even register for their honeymoons at willing travel agencies. Several

banks around the country offer a mortgage registry, designed to permit friends and family to help with payments on a couple's first home as a wedding gift. Floridians Jennifer Beber, an advertising executive, and David Frankel, an Oscar-winning filmmaker, devised another original plan. They registered with their gardener, so that friends could help them finance the landscaping of their new Miami residence. Instead of buying them three place settings, guests could call the landscaper and buy them three palm trees. Knowing that the plantings would grow along with the marriage was a great feeling, say family members.

As fun-filled as it may sound (who doesn't love to pick out presents?), registering can also be overwhelming. Here's how to make the process simpler:

• Consider registering at a variety of places: a traditional store for friends of parents who don't know you well and will feel comfortable choosing a vase or a place setting; a kitchen store for cookware and practical items; and a location that expresses your individual tastes or pursuits—perhaps a trendy department store, a smaller neighborhood shop where you've always admired the merchandise or the aforementioned spa or gym. You may also want to register in more than one city if your families are spread out.

Unique glassware, such as these blue tumblers with gold details, makes a lovely gift.

the feel of the store, then bring her fiancé or her mother on a second visit. Once some gifts have been purchased from the registry, you may want to return and add new items. Stores change their stock and floor displays every few months, and there are always new things to see.

● When registering, think about now and five years from now. Try to envision your future lifestyle and choose gifts that you will enjoy and use through the decades in addition to items that are simply the fashion of the day.

● Don't be shy. Let the bridal coordinator who is working with you know all your likes and dislikes. If you are hesitant to put an especially costly object on the registry, you can always add a note to your file. The coordinator will draw it to the attention of a guest who expresses interest in spending more money than any of the registered items cost.

● Let each registry know where else you have filed. Most stores are accommodating to brides, especially if the registry has been sold out and guests need to be directed to another location.

● Always make an appointment so that an experienced professional can walk you through the appropriate departments and procedures.

● Don't feel that you have to make all your decisions at once. One expert from the New York department store Barneys, which is renowned for its selection of exquisite table- and housewares, recommends that the bride go alone the first time to get

Giving and Receiving

MANY WOMEN ADMIT to becoming better gift givers themselves after they have their turn as a bride. "When you register, you get exactly what you want," says interior designer Victoria Hagan. "But when I really know the couple, I like to give something personal, something that I know will complement their home because I've been in it so many times." Sarah Medford, a *Town & Country* editor, agrees. "I give mono-

grammed napkin rings," she says. "It's a great way to start a family tradition." Medford buys a box of six, with the idea that the family will grow in size. She also likes to give antique napkin rings, each in a different pattern, so that every member of the family will have his or her own distinctive design. Blaine Trump favors monogrammed picture frames—and tries to include a picture of the bride and groom that

the couple has never seen. A gift relating to the couple's honeymoon also makes a memorable impact. *Town & Country* editor Melissa Biggs Bradley purchased barware etched with African animals for a couple who went to South Africa on their honeymoon, which was the honeymoon destination of Bradley and her husband. "I know that it was a good gift," she explains, "because we received it, too, and we love it."

One mother-in-law gave her daughter-in-law-to-be a handmade photo album of the groom as a baby. It was a personal and treasured gift.

Getting Personal

PLANNING MAY BE everything, but the surprise gift is the one that truly touches the bride and groom. Unless, of course, it's the psychedelic lamp shade from a well-meaning friend of the family. (Now that's a surprise of another sort.) Surprise gifts tend to be less practical and more indulgent and intimate than traditional ones.

Brides and guests alike worry that gifts from a registry might be impersonal. But even at the most traditional stores—Tiffany & Co., Cartier, Asprey & Garrard, Neiman Marcus, Bergdorf Goodman—the more conventional items, such as silver trays or frames, can be monogrammed, or inscribed according to the wishes of the gift giver to make them more

meaningful. One wedding guest, a close friend of both bride and groom, recently personalized a Cartier box by having it engraved with a map dotted with gemstones marking the places where the couple had traveled together. For the sentimental, there are other ideas, like a music box that plays their wedding song; some specialty stores will laminate a box with the wedding invitation or a picture of the couple. Even practical gifts can be luxurious. One bride obsessed with cleanliness, for instance, was reduced to tears of joy when she received a Miele vacuum. "It's the Mercedes-Benz of vacuums," she explains. "I'd always wanted one desperately."

Of course, there's always a year's worth of caviar and a monogrammed caviar holder. In fact, some businesses now specialize in sending a year's worth of just about anything to satisfy your personal cravings: caviar, tropical fruit, flowers, luxe baked goods, European chocolates and rare wines. Such a gift truly keeps on giving, because you will receive an installment each month.

Gift givers who are not convinced a registry is personal may still want to ask for your advice and suggestions. If someone requests ideas, don't be shy. People mean it when they ask for help. In this instance, it may be easier to express your interest in a gift that relates to a cultural, educational or philanthropic interest. Some couples believe these

E-mail simply won't suffice. Nor will a phone call. The thank-you note—four or five lines handwritten on informal stationery—is still a mainstay of wedding etiquette. Joy Lewis, the owner of Mrs. John Strong, a century-old stationery shop in Manhattan, believes that thank-you notes should be written while the present is still "fresh." The longer you wait, the harder it is to write the note. "Someone who sends you a present is dying to know if you received it and if you like it," she says. "They feel somewhat disappointed, maybe even a little rejected, when the note arrives two months later." Of course, if you receive a gift that really knocks your socks off, it's perfectly lovely to pick up the phone and thank the giver with enthusiasm, as long as the call is followed up with a note soon thereafter.

What has changed is who writes the note. Even though gifts are traditionally sent to the bride, grooms are now sending some of the thank-yous. Often, brides and grooms each have their own stationery printed for thank-you notes or have paper engraved with a joint monogram. No matter who is doing the writing, it is important to keep the voices straight, and it is not appropriate for one person to sign the other's name. If the bride writes the note, she should say something like, "Jack and I love the soup ladle you sent us . . ." and then sign her own name. Even though you are part of a couple, you should not presume to speak for the other person. The same goes for the groom.

guests to donate to their own choices. (Second-time brides who have already received their share of traditional gifts often request such donations in their names.) Instead of putting "in lieu of gifts" directly on the invitation, a week later send out a separate note that says something informal, such as: "You know how we feel about the American Cancer Society. . . . In lieu of wedding gifts, won't you please send a donation in our name?"

And do understand that people still may want to send wedding presents.

are the most personal gifts of all, especially when they reflect the shared interest of the giver and the recipient.

Here are some suggestions:

● Ask for a tree to be planted in your name. Many nature and park conservancies accept donations for trees, and also for park benches, and can install a plaque with the bride and groom's name.

● A family member may enjoy indulging an expressed interest in family lineage. A genealogist can trace a couple's individual family trees up to the point where they merge. When an artist draws it up and frames it, the mutual family tree makes a truly personal gift.

● Indulge your cultural passions. Some guests are delighted to give a subscription to the theater, opera or ballet. For a healthy donation to the institution, a private tour of the facility off-hours can sometimes be arranged.

● Suggest a gift to a favorite charity or ask

For the couple who has everything—plant a tree, or a grove of trees, in their names, or pledge to maintain a tree in a nearby park.

Wedding Style: Favorite Wedding Gifts

GIFT GIVING ENABLES people to be a lasting part of your life through the presents they bestow. The best way to enjoy the memories is to share them. Here is a look at the favorite gifts of some women recently married and some married a long time ago:

Melissa Biggs Bradley, *Town & Country*: A cousin who had been living in Cambodia brought us an antique lacquerware box that was hundreds of years old. And my aunt and uncle gave us the silver salt and pepper shakers that my father had given them as a wedding present. We were very touched by that.

Susan Fales-Hill, television producer: Actor and friend Geoffrey Holder gave us a painting he did especially for us. It was a forest scene depicting tiny figures walking as if on a journey. My uncle gave me the family silver. And my assistant gave me Tupperware, which, believe it or not, I use every day and appreciate so much.

Pamela Fiori, *Town & Country*: A pair of silver candelabra from friends who own the Four Seasons restaurant. At first we thought they were too splendid for us, but we sort of grew into them. They fit into our life and our dining room so perfectly now.

Victoria Hagan, interior designer: I received a silver mint julep cup that I love, and I actually enjoy it as a vase. I reinvented uses for a lot of our gifts because I like to use things in unexpected ways.

Evelyn Lauder, Estée Lauder Companies: Stanley Marcus of Neiman Marcus gave us an early eighteenth-century silver warming dish that I still use for all my buffets.

The silver candelabrum Pamela Fiori received as a wedding present. "At first we thought they were too splendid for us," she says, "but now they fit into our life and dining room so perfectly."

Mara Leighton, antique jewelry expert: We were given a beautiful hand-painted plate that one of my father's oldest friends commissioned. It incorporates different symbols of marriage, as well as our names and wedding date. Many of our guests also knew that I collect Art Deco objects; we received a beautiful silver teapot from France and a Deco watercolor of a New York cityscape.

Andrea Marcovicci, torch singer: I sensed that people delved into their own lives for our wedding presents. I was given a piece of sheet music signed by Craig Carnelia, a songwriter of days past. Ida and Ron Rifkin gave us a set of cranberry glasses that were exquisite. Friends of the family even gave us silver candlesticks, which had been in their family for a century.

Beth Minardi, beauty expert: Matching cashmere slippers and a coordinating cashmere throw. It was such a luxurious gift.

Sally Quinn, journalist: My husband gave me a beautiful necklace trimmed with gold filigree that was given to his great-great-grandfather by Napoleon Bonaparte's sister, Pauline. It's composed of turquoise mosaics about the size of silver dollars and features pictures of the Coliseum and the Pantheon in Rome. There are earrings to match. They date from 1815 and were given to me in the original box. I still wear them all the time.

Susan Rotenstreich, couture jewelry designer: Old silver goblets, which I adore and still use today. We received them from collective aunts and uncles in my family. Every time I take them out, it feels like the first time. They just take my breath away.

Jamie Tisch: A close friend commissioned an oil painting from our favorite painter, Stephen Hannock. An homage to Magritte, the work is a landscape showing trees and the sky at dusk; in the background you can see the ghost of my wedding invitation.

Blaine Trump, philanthropist: Silver flatware was a gift from my mother- and father-in-law. Every time I look at it, I smile and think of them and love it. I know it's a typical wedding present, but ours was a really old pattern, purchased at Christie's. Such a gift is everlasting. You have it forever and then pass it down to your children.

Lillian Wang von Stauffenberg, fashion observer: From my uncle, I got a pair of old Chinese lamps that I adore. They're classic blue-and-white antique Chinese pottery, which I collect. He also sent me the poem that my grandfather wrote and read at my wedding.

Sylvia Weinstock, cake baker: Ben, my husband, was probably my favorite wedding gift. I was married in 1949. In those days, who had any money? I think my second favorite wedding gift was actually a set of pots with copper bottoms. I used them until they fell apart.

Stacey Okun, *Town & Country*: My honeymoon. My husband planned the whole thing: a trip starting out in the South of France, driving through Provence and ending in Paris. He put into it the care that I put into planning the wedding and was so concerned about every detail. As wonderful as the trip was, the best part for me was going through American customs on the way home and getting to declare ourselves a family on the customs card.

Town & Country
Pamela Fiori, Editor-in-Chief
Mary Shanahan, Creative Director

Produced by Welcome Enterprises, Inc. and Fair Street Productions

H. Clark Wakabayashi and Susan Wechsler, Project Directors
Gregory Wakabayashi, Designer
Deborah Anderson/Photosearch, Inc., Photo Editor

Library of Congress Cataloging-in-Publication Data available.

10 9 8 7 6 5 4 3 2 1

First Paperback Edition 2004
Published by Hearst Books
A Division of Sterling Publishing Co., Inc.
387 Park Avenue South, New York, NY 10016

Town & Country is a trademark owned by Hearst Magazines
Property, Inc., in USA, and Hearst Communications, Inc., in
Canada. Hearst Books is a trademark owned by Hearst
Communications, Inc.

www.townandcountrymag.com

Distributed in Canada by Sterling Publishing
c/o Canadian Manda Group, One Atlantic Avenue, Suite 105
Toronto, Ontario, Canada M6K 3E7

Distributed in Australia by Capricorn Link (Australia) Pty. Ltd.
P.O. Box 704, Windsor, NSW 2756 Australia

Printed in China

ISBN 1-58816-377-6

The producers wish to thank all the wonderful photographers,
wedding planners, designers, caterers, and especially the brides
and grooms who so graciously went out of their way to meet
our requests.

ILLUSTRATION CREDITS:

Cover: Miki Duisterhof; *Back cover:* MichellePattee.com;
Spine: Holger Thoss; *1:* Thayer Allyson Gowdy,
littlewhitedress.com; *2:* Oberto Gili; *4:* Mallory Samson,
www.mallorysamson.com, New York City & Sausalito, CA;
6: Ronny Jaques; *10–11:* Courtesy of Colin Cowie Lifestyle.
Photograph by Nadine Froger; *12:* Miki Duisterhof; *13:* Tanya
Malott Lawson, tanya.com; *14:* Thayer Allyson Gowdy,
littlewhitedress.com; *15:* Thayer Allyson Gowdy,
littlewhitedress.com; *17:* Marc Royce; *18:* Courtesy of Laurie
Arons Special Events. Photograph © Eliot Holtzman;
20: Courtesy of Laurie Arons Special Events. Photo © Eliot
Holtzman; *21:* Matt Mendelsohn; *22:* © Mia Matheson; *23:* Mallory
Samson, www.mallorysamson.com, New York City & Sausalito,
CA; *24–25:* Courtesy of Laurie Arons Special Events, Stanlee R.
Gatti Designs, Tents by Stuart Rentals. Photograph by Aengus
McGiffin; *26–27:* Kaija Berzins Braus; *28:* Courtesy of Laurie
Arons Special Events, Stanlee R. Gatti Designs. Photograph by
Roger Olson, Los Angeles; *29 Top:* Courtesy of Laurie Arons
Special Events. Photograph © Eliot Holtzman; *29 Bottom:* Marc
Royce; *30:* Terry Gruber Photography; *31:* Luca Trovato;
32: Courtesy of Laurie Arons Special Events. Photograph by Russell
Photography Group, www.russellphoto.com; *33 Top:* Courtesy of
Ferree Florsheim, Chicago. Photograph by Joel Schachtel;
33 Bottom: Courtesy of Laurie Arons Special Events; Photograph
© Eliot Holtzman; *34–35:* Julie Skarratt; *36:* Courtesy of Ferree
Florsheim, Chicago. Photograph by Stuart–Rodgers Ltd; *37:* Courtesy
of Philip Baloun; *38:* Julie Skarratt; *39 Top:* Courtesy of Laurie Arons
Special Events. Photograph © Eliot Holtzman; *39 Bottom:* Mary
Hilliard; *40:* Luca Trovato; *41:* Courtesy of Just Ask Peter, Aspen.
Alice Koelle Photography; *42:* Courtesy of Laurie Arons Special
Events. Photograph © russell/harrison photography; *43:* Courtesy
of Laurie Arons Special Events, Stanlee R. Gatti Designs, Tents
by Stuart Rentals. Photo by Dennis Hearne; *44–45:* Julie
Skarratt; *46:* Philippe Cheng; *47:* Courtesy of Paula Le Duc
Fine Catering, San Francisco. Photograph by Joshua Ets–Hokin;
48: Courtesy of Laurie Arons Special Events. Photograph
© russell/harrison photography; *49:* Julie Skarratt; *50:* Courtesy
of Stanlee R. Gatti Designs. Photograph by Kathleen Harrison
for Michellepattee.com; *51:* Courtesy of Paula Le Duc Fine
Catering, San Francisco. Photograph by Todd Pickering;
52 Top Left: Courtesy of Laurie Arons Special Events,
Stanlee R. Gatti Designs. Photograph © Eliot Holtzman;
52 Bottom Right: Courtesy of Paula Le Duc Fine Catering, San
Francisco. Photograph by Robert Bengston; *52 Bottom Left:* Sarah
Merians Photography; *52 Top Right:* Courtesy of Creative Edge
Parties; *53:* Courtesy of Paula Le Duc Fine Catering, San
Francisco. Photograph by Todd Pickering; *55:* Thayer Allyson
Gowdy, littlewhitedress.com; *56–57:* Denis Reggie with Philip
Gould; *58:* Tanya Malott Lawson, tanya.com; *59:* Courtesy of
Creative Edge Parties; *60:* Courtesy of Just Ask Peter, Aspen.
Alice Koelle Photography; *61:* Courtesy of Just Ask Peter,

Acknowledgments

WRITING A BOOK CAN BE a lot like having a baby, and in this particular case, I managed to do both simultaneously. Unlike a pregnancy, however, an evolving book can take dozens of people (and certainly more than nine months!) to nurture it to completion. It is these people I must thank here.

First and foremost, I owe a tremendous debt of gratitude to Pamela Fiori, who has given me so many broadening and wonderful opportunities since I joined her staff at *Town & Country* in 1994. She has graciously accommodated my ever-changing lifestyle while continuing to offer me substantial and fulfilling work. Pamela is an inspiration to me—in style and in substance.

Other staff members, past and present, have kindly held my hand through this project, let me pick their brains, rummage through their own wedding memories and borrow their precious sources. They are my dear friend, Margot Frankel, the talented Melissa Biggs Bradley, Sarah Medford, Jane Agnew, the ever-patient Tracy Gold, Mike Cannon, John Cantrell, and most important, the supremely creative—and always calm—Mary Shanahan. Susan Rogoski's brilliant editing on my previous articles for the magazine and Leslie Barber's superb copy editing stayed fresh in my mind as I wrote this book. Melissa Milrad Goldstein provided top-notch research assistance when it was most needed. Betty Rice at Hearst Books has been a most patient and reassuring editor, and I have appreciated her interest in my children as well as in my deadlines. Rachel Carley edited with a deft hand, giving my voice a chance to be heard. After too many months alone with this book,

the team at Welcome Enterprises and Fair Street Productions were a most helpful addition. Clark Wakabayashi and Susan Wechsler put the process on a smooth course to production, and Gregory Wakabayashi's beautiful design could not have been more appropriate for the subject matter. They deserve much of the credit for making sure this project came to fruition. Deborah Anderson, of Photosearch, scoured the country for the perfect pictures and ensured that today's top-notch wedding photographers were given a voice in this book. Lauren Picker, my colleague and so much more, provided support, advice and humor via e-mail and lit a fire under me at a very crucial point in the writing process. I am eternally grateful for her friendship. Lori Kase has always been there for me, in spirit and in person, and I suspect she always will be.

Wedding planners across the country were my lifeline to the world of wonderful weddings during the research phase of this book. Despite their incredibly hectic schedules, they still managed to consult with me via their cell phones and car phones. Laurie Arons of San Francisco, Mindy Weiss and Frankie Berger of Los Angeles and Elizabeth Allen were especially generous with both their time and their tales. As for the unbelievably creative, vivacious and adorable Marcy Blum, whom I have been interviewing about weddings for years: If I were getting married all over again, I'd hire her; if I were a man, I'd marry her immediately.

The brides (and grooms), newlyweds and long-married couples who have shared their love stories with me for this book will forever hold a special place in my heart. I must especially thank Valerie Rozen and Summer Tompkins Walker, whose inspirational weddings could form the basis of their own books; Ellen Katz, a graceful second-time bride; Laura Fisher, Cynthia Rowley, Carla Ruben-Avramopoulos, Carolina Herrera, Brooke Astor, Andrea Marcovicci, Alix Toub, Suzie Tompkins, Kendal and Gary Friedman, Susan Fales-Hill, Lillian Wang von Stauffenberg, Courtnay Duchin, Nicole Dawes, Judith Leiber, Evelyn Lauder, Lynn Gosman, Joan Hunter, Kim and Ralph Rosenberg, Carol Brodie Gelles, Blaine Trump, Candy Scraber, the incredibly supportive Linda and Henry Dunay; Jessica and Mark Mindich; and Laurence and Carolyn Belfer, the most interested and encouraging of friends.

Many other sources provided great insights and exciting glimpses into the behind-the-scenes preparations for weddings. There isn't enough space here to thank all the florists, caterers, dressmakers, designers, cake bakers, photographers, musicians, makeup artists and others. They will see their ideas on the previous pages and, I hope, know how much I appreciate their letting me tag along, ask personal questions, pore through their photo albums and borrow from their memory banks. That said, some individuals were so incredibly helpful—and dear—that they must be mentioned by name. They are the charming Monica Hickey, Vanessa Noel, Bill Hamilton, Amy Rice, Pat Kerr, Bill Blass, Stephen Knoll, Carmine and Beth Minardi, Bobbi Brown, Nikki Padula and Liz Michael for their fashion and beauty expertise; the inimitable James de Givenchy, Mara and Fred Leighton, Gabrielle Sanchez, Cynthia Wolff, Susan Rotenstreich and Renee Lewis for jewelry advice; Letitia Baldrige on etiquette; Susan Florsheim and Paula Le Duc, who provided ample food for thought; Sylvia Weinstock, Betty Baird, Cecile Gady and Linda Goldsheft, cake-makers extraordinaire; Peter Duchin, Mark Stevens and Michael Carney for wise words on music; Stanlee Gatti, Philip Baloun, Renny Reynolds, Colin Cowie, Martha Harris and Bill Tansey for guidance on flowers and wedding design; Ellen Weldon, Joy Lewis and Luke Pontifell for invitations advice; and Denis Reggie, Julie Skarratt, Terry Gruber, Tony Artz and Nate Weil for information on photography and videography.

After writing *Elegant Weddings*, I know that there are many, many good husbands out there. But none as good as mine. I dedicate this book to Eric, who got down on bended knee one hot, romantic July morning in Venice and changed my life forever. I thank him for somehow surviving our wedding (and the writing of this wedding book) intact. I am most blessed and most proud to be his wife. My parents—doting, devoted, dear and incredibly beloved—have always tried to make all my dreams come true. My wedding was but one of those dreams. Not a day goes by when I don't thank my lucky stars for their impact on my life, from their writing of *Why the Sea Is Salty* to their impeccable care of my children. One of the pleasures of writing this book (and at times, the only pleasure) was to know that I could dedicate it to them. Finally, the first two offspring of my marriage, Russell and Daniel, must also be given credit. They add a richness to my life and my marriage that I never knew could exist—even when one of them repeatedly pressed buttons on my computer, wiping away entire afternoons of work.

STACEY OKUN

Index